100

THINGS TO DO IN THE

QUAD CITIES

BEFORE YOU

DIE

12/1/22

Chris —
Happy adventuring!

Jonath

Photo courtesy of Quad City Botanical Center

100

THINGS TO DO IN THE
QUAD CITIES
BEFORE YOU
DIE

• •

JONATHAN TURNER

Library of Congress Control Number: 2022937000

ISBN: 9781681063928

Design by Jill Halpin

Front cover photo courtesy of the River Room.

Printed in the United States of America
22 23 24 25 26   5 4 3 2 1

CONTENTS

• •

Music and Entertainment

● ●

Culture and History

• •

• •

PREFACE

In an 1886 interview with the *Chicago Tribune*, Mark Twain spoke of one of his muses: "It is strange how little has been written about the Upper Mississippi. The river below St. Louis has been described time and again, and it is the least interesting part . . . Along the Upper Mississippi, every hour brings something new. There are crowds of odd islands, bluffs, prairies, hills, woods and villages—everything one could desire to amuse the children. Few people ever think of going there, however."

Life on the Mississippi has certainly changed since Twain's time, not least because many people think of visiting and moving here. My wife and I did, in 1995—to the Quad Cities, on the Upper Mississippi, on the border between Illinois and Iowa—and so much has changed and improved in that time. The QC is a singular metropolitan area not only along the mighty Big Muddy, but a unique region nationwide. We're a bi-state area with one city larger than the rest (Davenport, Iowa), but the Illinois and Iowa sides of the river are equal in location of amazing visitor attractions and amenities. We're an unusual area in that the river runs not north to south (as in most of its length) but east to west—giving the name Bent River or River Bend you'll see in the area.

This region of 400,000-plus people has all the friendliness, affordability, and short, headache-free commutes of many small towns, but the tremendous variety and quality of things to do of many big cities. This book lists 100 of them for you, and it was a true challenge to limit myself to only 100.

While by the time we moved here, downtown Moline had its new arena, Rock Island had its dinner theater, and Davenport had its grand concert hall, so much has grown and developed to add to this delicious menu of offerings—innovative, independently owned restaurants and bars, live-music venues, theater companies, museums, galleries, parks, and the list goes on. The QC technically refers to four cities (Davenport, Moline, Rock Island, and Bettendorf), but this book covers many more beyond these borders. And growing East Moline (particularly the area called "the Bend") has long proclaimed on its welcome sign, "One of the Quad Cities."

So welcome to the bounty and beauty throughout this remarkable region—from natural wonders to the wonderful things you can do all year-round. My sincere thanks in preparation of this book goes to Visit Quad Cities (which has helped me every step of the way), and the fine folks at Reedy Press for supporting me in the process.

visitquadcities.com

Photo courtesy of Bix Bistro

FOOD AND DRINK

CHOOSE FROM 100 INTOXICATING BREWS
AT ARMORED GARDENS

If you can't find a beer to your liking at Armored Gardens bar and restaurant in downtown Davenport, it likely doesn't exist. The truly friendly confines contains a mind-blowing 100 beers on tap, which are rotated and feature many selections from local and regional craft breweries. You can find everything from a peanut-butter milk stout from Colorado, breakfast stout from Michigan, dunkle with peaches and pecans from Texas, and Moose Drool ale from Montana, to Bikini Bottom Pineapple Wheat from Bettendorf's Five Cities, and Mango Me Hoppy IPA from LeClaire's Green Tree. Creative cocktails and affordable wines are also available, with a supremely tasty food menu.

315 Pershing Ave., Davenport, IA, 563-345-1000
armoredgardens.com

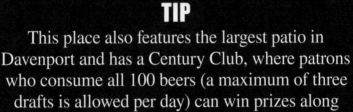

TIP

This place also features the largest patio in Davenport and has a Century Club, where patrons who consume all 100 beers (a maximum of three drafts is allowed per day) can win prizes along the way, with an AG hoodie as the top keepsake.

LAP UP CULINARY LUXURY
AT DUCK CITY BISTRO

As downtown Davenport has transformed itself over the years, there's been one consistent culinary mainstay. Duck City Bistro, across from an equally beloved institution, the Adler Theatre, provides plush, romantic elegance and outstanding food and drink, as it has since 1991. Jeremy Moskowitz, the chef/co-owner, was named chef of the year in 2020 by the Iowa Restaurant Association. He's been executive chef of Duck City for over 20 years and has owned the restaurant since 2012, when his father, Charles, handed over the business. The bistro is a popular destination for PGA golfers during the John Deere Classic, including Pat Perez, who orders the same thing every time (stuffed pork chop).

115 E 3rd St., Davenport, IA, 563-322-3825
duckcitybistro.co

TIP

One of my favorites is a twist on filet mignon—
the Filet Melissa, a charbroiled steak topped with
braised vidalia onion and a delicate cream Brie
cheese sauce, served with candied corkscrew
bacon and steamed asparagus.

SAVOR
SWEET NOSTALGIA
AT LAGOMARCINO'S

When you step inside the warm, inviting Lagomarcino's (in either its Moline or Davenport locations), you're literally entering a simpler, sweeter time. Since 1908, Lagomarcino's has treated the Quad Cities to its famous homemade chocolates, candies, ice cream, and other delectable treats. Founded by an Italian immigrant family, the confectionery business now employs the fourth generation of the family, and Lago's (as it's known) is famous for its irresistible hot fudge sundaes and its homey, welcoming vibe. Originating in downtown Moline with its handcrafted mahogany booths and original copper kettle kitchen, it opened a delightful, bright and cheery second location in the Village of East Davenport in 1997.

2132 E 11th St., Davenport, IA, 563-324-6137
1422 5th Ave., Moline, IL, 309-764-1814
lagomarcinos.com

MORE TO SATISFY
YOUR SWEET TOOTH IN THE QUAD CITIES

Oh So Sweet by Tiphanie
They provide the best, freshest homemade bakery items (everything made from scratch) that the QC has to offer, such as cupcakes, cakes, cookies, bars, and whoopie pies, to name a few.
314 Main St., Davenport, IA, 563-345-YUMM
ohsosweetbytiphanie.com

Cookies & Dreams
This heavenly place is more than just really great cookies. They are about joy, connection, celebration, and never giving up on your dream.
217 E 2nd St., Davenport, IA, 563-424-1940
6768 Competition Dr., Bettendorf, IA, 563-449-2588
idreamaboutcookies.com

Shameless Chocoholic
If there's something appropriate to be smothered in chocolate, these sweet wizards have done it. In two delectable locations, find everything handmade from truffles, caramels, and butter creams to sugar-free treats.
1526 River Dr., Moline, IL, 309-524-4201
101 S Cody Rd., LeClaire, IA, 563-289-1339
shamelesschocoholic.com

Chocolate Manor
More unique hand-crafted creations for any confection.
110 E 2nd St., Davenport, IA, 563-355-6600
chocolatemanorchocolates.com

SAMPLE CRAFT BEER
ON THE QC ALE TRAIL

There's little as satisfying or uniquely QC as enjoying a Cherry
Bomb Blonde on the outdoor deck of the Front Street Taproom at
Davenport's Freight House complex, or a Hop Along Casually on
the patio of Green Tree Brewery in downtown LeClaire, both of
which you can chase down with superb views of the Mississippi.
Like most cities across the country, the craft brewing craze is
booming here, and the QC Ale Trail is a fun, productive way to
track your exercise among nearly 20 local brew locations (Front
Street, the oldest craft brew pub in Iowa, and Bent River Brewing
Co. have two spots each). From Geneseo to Muscatine, you can
earn a free bottle opener after you visit four or more breweries,
and get a free pint glass when you complete the trail.

qcaletrail.com

TIP
You can create a mobile passport and join the Facebook group to share
progress and favorite beers as you blaze the tasty trail.

SAMPLE CRAFT BEER ON THE QC ALE TRAIL

Bent River Brewing Co.
1413 5th Ave., Moline, IL
309-797-2722
bentriverbrewing.com

Blue Cat Brewing Company
113 18th St., Rock Island, IL
309-558-6063
bluecatbrewingco.com

Crawford Brew Works
3659 Devils Glen Rd.
Bettendorf, IA, 563-332-0243
crawfordbrewworks.com

Five Cities Brewing
2255 Falcon Ave., Bettendorf, IA
563-232-6105
fivecitiesbrewing.com

Front Street Pub & Eatery
208 E River Dr., Davenport, IA
563-322-1569
frontstreetbrew.com

Galena Brewing Company
1534 River Dr., Moline, IL
309-524-3148
galenabrewery.com

Geneseo Brewing Co.
102 S State St., Geneseo, IL
309-945-1422
geneseobrewing.com

Great Revivalist Brew Lab
1225 S Oakwood Ave.
Geneseo, IL, 309-944-5466
greatrevivalist.com

Green Tree Brewery
309 N Cody Rd., Le Claire, IA
563-729-1164
greentreebrewery.com

Midwest Ale Works
537 12th Ave., East Moline, IL
309-751-4600
maw.beer

Nerdspeak Brewery
7563 State St., Bettendorf, IA
563-232-1037
nerdspeakbrewery.com

Radicle Effect Brewerks
1340 31st St., Rock Island, IL
309-283-7605
rebrewerks.com

Rebellion Brew Haus
529 3rd Avenue A, Moline, IL
309-517-1684
rebellionbrewhaus.com

Stompbox Brewing
210 E River Dr., Davenport, IA
563-424-1237
stompboxbrewing.com

RELAX WITH COMFORT FOOD
AT QC COFFEE & PANCAKE HOUSE

This is a popular breakfast and lunch spot for many reasons. Chiefly, the food is darned delicious and the staff super friendly. Located in downtown Rock Island across from Circa '21, the culinary wizards Jose and Sarah Zepeda have owned and operated it since 2013. Jose has been in the restaurant industry over 20 years and has won many People's Choice awards. They are passionate, and as a family-run business, it's clear that superb customer service is a priority—their customers regularly leave happier than when they arrived. Some of my favorites on the huge, bountiful menu include the Koffee Break Skillet (two eggs with bacon strips, sausage, ham, mushrooms, green peppers, onions, tomato, and cheese), the Reuben sandwich, and their gigantic gyro. Home of the famous Cinnamon Roll Pancake, the house's menu has a mouth-watering variety of omelets, egg sandwiches, skillets, other breakfasts, salads, burgers, and classic lunch sandwiches.

1831 3rd Ave., Rock Island, IL, 309-788-9589
qccoffeeandpancakehouse.com

TASTE BITES AND DRINKS WITH A VIEW
AT UP SKYBAR AND RIVER ROOM

There are two spectacular rooftop bars in the QC. The first is the sleek, stunning River Room, on the ninth floor of the Hyatt Place/Hyatt House Quad Cities in East Moline. The spacious lounge features breathtaking views of the Mississippi River and perhaps the best spot to watch the sunset in the area. Its eclectic menu features local craft beers from the QC Ale Trail and a wide variety of wines and cocktails. The River Room light bites (including dips, appetizers, and flatbread pizzas) are served Thursdays, Fridays, and Saturdays. In downtown Davenport, the UP Skybar is on top of the stylish Current Iowa (originally designed by renowned architect Daniel Burnham as Davenport's first hotel). UP showcases both indoor and outdoor seating, and the patio also affords commanding views of the river. Some tables have their own firepits. The appetizers and drinks on the menu are equally creative and delicious.

The River Room
111 Bend Blvd., East Moline, IL, 309-278-4790
riverroombar.com

The UP Skybar
215 N Main St., Davenport, IA, 563-231-9555
thecurrentiowa.com/dining

GET YOUR MORNING BUZZ
AT 392CAFFÉ

The coffee craze has taken off in the QC in a big way, as locally driven shops have proliferated in recent years as a staggeringly creative antidote to Starbucks and convenience-store brews. The highest profile may be the upscale 392Caffé—co-founded in 2019 by Davenport native and WWE wrestling champ Seth Rollins, connected in downtown Davenport to his wrestling academy. It has expanded to three locations. The 392Caffé's menu includes baked goodies, cold and hot drinks, blended beverages, smoothie bowls, sandwiches, a toast bar, and power bowls. Each dine-in drink seems a work of art.

502 W 3rd St., Davenport, IA, 563-275-6292
4750 Utica Ridge Rd., Davenport, IA, 563-265-1290
216 S 2nd St., Clinton, IA, 563-484-0392
392caffe.com

OTHER SUPERB COFFEE DESTINATIONS IN THE QC INCLUDE

Redband Coffee Company
329 E 4th St., Davenport, IA
110 W 13th St., Davenport, IA
(drive-thru), 563-484-0098
redbandcoffee.com

Milltown
3800 River Dr., Moline, IL
1025 Utica Ridge Pl.
Bettendorf, IA, 309-517-6444
milltowncoffeeco.com

Awake Coffee Company
1430 4th Ave., Rock Island, IL
309-558-0124

Iron & Grain
585 12th Ave., East Moline, IL
309-429-3404
1618 N Main St., Davenport, IA
563-900-4766
1275 Avenue of the Cities
Silvis, IL, 309-798-4354
irongraincoffee.com

Cool Beanz Coffeehouse
512 24th St., Rock Island, IL
309-558-0909
coolbeanzcoffeehouse.com

Dead Poets Espresso
1525 3rd Ave. A, Moline, IL
309-736-7606
`deadpoetsespresso.com

BREW in the Village
1104 Jersey Ridge Rd.
Davenport, IA, 563-424-1902
brewinthevillage.com

Atomic Coffee Bar
4707 N Brady St., Davenport, IA
503-686-5055
atomiccoffeebar.com

Coffee Apothecary
2751 53rd Ave., Bettendorf, IA
563-349-7757
facebook.com/coffeeapothecaryqc

Coffee Hound
3451 Devils Glen Rd.
Bettendorf, IA, 563-449-0030
5141 Competition Dr. (at TBK Complex), Bettendorf, IA
563-232-8366
qccoffeehound.com

GET A LICK UP
WITH THE WONDERS
OF WHITEY'S ICE CREAM

Another delectable QC institution, Whitey's Ice Cream has been serving heaven in a cup or cone since 1933. Though its iconic red-and-white logo is instantly recognizable here, its name comes from founder Chester Lindgren, nicknamed "Whitey" due to his blond hair. In 1935, Lindgren hired 15-year-old Bob Tunberg, who worked for him throughout high school and for years after. Tunberg bought the business in 1953 and it has stayed in his family. Also sold in local grocery stores, Whitey's is known for extra-thick shakes and malts, which can be held upside down without spilling. Some of my favorite flavors are Strawberry Cheesecake, Graham Central Station, and Sgt. Camo, a camouflage-colored ice cream made from Graham crackers, marshmallow ice cream, and Whitey's fudge.

TIP

All profits from the sale of Sgt. Camo are donated to military veterans groups, and the ice cream has been sent to the Pentagon and to military personnel and their families.

WHITEY'S ICE CREAM LOCATIONS

1601 Avenue of the Cities, Moline, IL, 309-762-4335

2601 41st St., Moline, IL, 309-762-4548

2520 18th Ave., Rock Island, IL, 309-788-5948

1335 Avenue of the Cities, East Moline, IL, 309-755-4313

1230 W Locust St., Davenport, IA, 563-322-0828

3515 Middle Rd., Bettendorf, IA, 563-332-4189

2419 E 53rd St., Davenport, IA, 563-359-0001

114 N 1st St., Eldridge, IA, 563-285-4141

whiteysicecream.com

RAISE A GLASS
AT WIDE RIVER WINERY

The gorgeous Wide River Winery is worth a day trip to Clinton, Iowa, where they have a 10-acre vineyard (and of course, a great river view) producing both red and white grape varietals. Luckily, they also have elegant tasting rooms (with inviting patios) in LeClaire and the Village of East Davenport and fun names like Felony Red, Ms. D'Meanor White, Caught Red Handed, and White Collar Crime.

1776 E Deer Creek Rd., Clinton, IA, 563-519-9463
106 N Cody Rd., LeClaire, IA, 563-289-2509
1128 Mound St., Davenport, IA, 563-888-5379
wideriverwinery.com

TIP
Nearby in downtown LeClaire, stop by the excellent Mississippi River Distilling Company, where they hand-craft (with local grains) a stunning variety of whiskey, gin, vodka, bourbon, rye, cocktails and cream liqueur, plus limited and seasonal releases. Their Celebration Center hosts private events—next to the distillery and Cocktail House, it's got amazing river views, a rooftop patio, and whiskey cellar. 303 N Cody Rd., LeClaire, IA, 563-484-4342, mrdistilling.com

16

TAKE A BREAK WITH IOWA STEAK
AT BASS STREET CHOP HOUSE

The Hawkeye State is well-known for producing prime cuts of beef. One of my favorite things in life is a tender, hot, medium-rare steak and you can't go wrong at several places in the Quad Cities. Chief among them is the stellar Bass Street Chop House in downtown Moline. It specializes in the finest cuts of hand-selected USDA prime and USDA choice dry aged cuts (chops) of meat. With a great river view, next to the Radisson on John Deere Commons, the elegant restaurant also features fresh seafood. The full-service Chop Bar has signature cocktails and an impressive single-malt scotch and bourbon selection, while the Chop Bar menu is perfect for those looking for lighter fare or late-night comestibles.

1425 River Dr., Moline, IL, 309-762-4700
bassstreetchophouse.com

TIP
You can find more delectable steaks in the area at Johnny's Italian Steakhouse (just across River Drive in Moline), as well as the Combine in East Moline, Tappa's Steakhouse, and Mo Brady's Steakhouse in Davenport.

SAVOR SLICES OF QC-STYLE PIZZA
AT FRANK'S AND HARRIS

While the QC is only 165 miles from Chicago, its pizzas are not deep-dish clones of the Windy City. As created by local classics Frank's (founded in 1955) and Harris (started in 1960), QC-style pies are unique in crust, sauce, sausage, assembly, and cut. The crust is flavored with malt syrup or molasses and is softer overall. "Zesty" and "spicy" are often used to describe a QC-style pizza sauce. The tomato sauce is spiced with red pepper flakes and ground cayenne to create a unique kick. Finely crumbled sausage on the pizzas make them super flavorful. A dense layer of lean Italian pork sausage, usually seasoned with fennel, covers any sausage QC-style pizza. The cheese is piled on top, and typically QC pizzas are sliced in narrow rectangles, not triangles.

Frank's Pizzeria
711 1st Ave., Silvis, IL, 309-755-0625

Harris Pizza
3903 14th Ave., Rock Island, IL, 309-788-3446
2520 18th St., Bettendorf, IA
524 E Locust St., Davenport, IA
harrispizza.com

TWO FOR MORE QC-STYLE PIZZA

Two of the other big names in local pizza are longtime institution Happy Joe's and newer, passionate upstart Lopiez. Started in 1972 by the irrepressible, beloved Joe Whitty (1937–2019) to put pizzas and ice cream in one place, Bettendorf-based Happy Joe's has over 40 locations, mainly in the Midwest. Its signature 'zas include BBQ, taco, combo, Hawaiian, Canadian bacon and sauerkraut, meatworks and vegetarian. The big menu also has pastas, sandwiches, soups, salads, appetizers, and morning offerings.

Lopiez began in 2019, highlighting New York-style slices, with many creative recipes, and it's got three QC locations, two in Davenport and one in Moline. Its creative pizzas include one named after Rock Island Arsenal with pepperoni, sausage, ham, bacon, mozzarella, mushrooms, black olives, tomatoes, green peppers, onion, artichoke hearts, and spinach. Both businesses are very community-minded, with many philanthropic partnerships.

Happy Joe's
2430 Spruce Hills Dr., Bettendorf, IA, 563-359-5457
happyjoes.com

Lopiez
429 E 3rd St., Ste. 1, Davenport, IA, 563-424-1130
2832 Brady St., Davenport, IA, 563-324-1269
1405 5th Ave., Moline, IL, 309-764-7644
lopiezpizza.com

GET ON TRACK
WITH HISTORIC CAFÉ D'MARIE

In 2009, Dr. DeAnna Marie Walter and Rick Kimmel (owner/chef) opened their beautiful circa-1865 home to the world as Café d'Marie. Tucked away in the Gold Coast/Hamburg historic district, off the railroad tracks near downtown Davenport, their home has become a serene home-away-from-home for many. The cozy restaurant is not only a visual delight, but the hand-crafted, tasty dishes are works of art in their own right. Café d'Marie offers breakfast and lunch menu options that are filling and healthy, including a dazzling variety of about 17 paninis, each made with artisan bread, perfectly grilled and topped with fresh spinach. The restaurant features specialty coffees, quiches, fresh homemade soup, salads, organic whole-leaf teas, and all-fruit smoothies. Café d'Marie is touted by families from all over the world as a unique getaway for family and friends and a favorable respite from hectic daily life, with an enticing European flair.

614 W 5th St., Davenport, IA, 563-323-3293
cafedmarie.com

SERVE YOURSELF
AT DIVERSE POUR BROS. TAPROOM

If you don't have the patience to get the attention of a bartender, Pour Bros. Taproom in Moline has the answer. The unique, friendly bar opened in early 2022 next to the Element Hotel, and is the third in a series of Pour Bros.—the first self-serve bar in Illinois. They also have locations in Peoria Heights and Champaign, Illinois. Patrons use a debit or credit card to get a Pour Bros. card that you scan at each self-serve tap, and customers pour whatever amount they want, within 1/10 of an ounce. Each of 28 taps (including wine and hard cider) is topped with a tablet that shows what the drink is, where it's from, price per ounce, alcoholic content, and if you tap the screen, you can get more detailed information. It's a delightfully freeing concept, and the owners feature beers made not only throughout the QC, but also in Iowa and Illinois.

1209 4th Ave., Ste. 2, Moline, IL, 309-517-3091
pourbrosmoline.com

FIND THE HEART OF AMERICA
AT MACHINE SHED AND MORE

If you want comfort food, you'll find it at Iowa Machine Shed in northwest Davenport. In 1978, the Heart of America Group opened the first Machine Shed on the outskirts of Davenport. Today there are six of the brand, in Iowa, Minnesota, and Wisconsin. The bountiful menu includes a wide range of desserts, topped by the signature apple dumpling, served hot with cinnamon ice cream. The Heart of America Group owns hotels, restaurants, and commercial development. Since its Machine Shed start, it has added many establishments to the portfolio, all of which are in the QC area, including Thunder Bay Grille, Johnny's Italian Steakhouse, Fifth Avenue Syndicate, Gramma's Kitchen & Checkered Flag, and the J Bar. From homey to stylishly upscale, these places all hit the spot for satisfying food and beverages, with outstanding customer service.

7250 Northwest Blvd., Davenport, IA, 563-391-2427
machineshed.com/davenport
heartofamericagroup.com

TIP

The latest QC addition, Moline's Fifth Avenue Syndicate, is attached to the Axis Hotel, a swanky bar and restaurant. 1630 5th Ave., Moline, IL, 309-640-0070, fifthavenuesyndicate.com

---

TAKE A JOYFUL RIDE
AT ME & BILLY

Billy Collins is a big, boisterous, bear of a man who loves to laugh. His downtown Davenport restaurant, Me & Billy Kitchen and Bar, has that same life-affirming, exuberant spirit. Named after the little boat Billy and his brother David used to ride out on a lake in northwest Iowa, the friendly, laid-back vibe of the restaurant is matched by the big, adventurous, and immensely satisfying menu. You can build your own burger with a tantalizing list of toppings, and two of the best sandwiches are the thin-shaved ribeye steak (with bacon horseradish mayo, arugula, Muenster cheese, and whiskey-glazed onion, on *pane Toscano* bread) and a Deluxe Darn Big Grilled Cheese (with cheddar and Muenster cheeses, whiskey-glazed onions, bacon-onion marmalade, tomato, spinach, and tomato basil sauce, on sourdough bread). Like Billy, the flavors are big and hearty.

200 W 3rd St., Davenport, IA, 563-323-1195
meandbilly.com

GET A TASTE OF CAJUN STYLE
AT BAYSIDE BISTRO

This Black, veteran-owned business has affection and respect baked into every delicious dish it offers. Owned by Army vet LaTisha Howlett and her husband, Navy vet Darryl, Bayside Bistro is no ordinary sandwich and smoothie shop. There's no deli meat on their menu. They use fresh ingredients, all items are made-to-order from scratch, and the menu specializes in New Orleans-style and Caribbean dishes such as po' boy sandwiches, pan-seared crab cakes, sautéed shrimp and andouille sausage, Caribbean pineapple chicken, and more. Their veggie burger alone is made with nine different veggies, and you can choose from 10 freshly made smoothies and nine cold-press juices. LaTisha prides herself on providing a home-style atmosphere and a big part of that feeling is being treated to anything she cooks up in her creative kitchen.

1105 Christie St., Ste. A, Village of East Davenport, IA, 563-277-8042
2704 18th Ave., Rock Island, IL, 309-468-8028
baysidebistroqc.com

BEGIN YOUR MEXICAN JOURNEY
AT LOS AGAVES

The QC is home to a strong and growing Mexican American population, and fittingly, many great Mexican restaurants. On the top of your list should be Los Agaves, a family-owned business that's been serving the area since 2004. It's got a huge menu of authentic Mexican food, freshly prepared every morning. Along with its house signature margaritas, they have a full bar in each of three QC locations. One of my favorite dishes is the Ranchero Chef's Special: tender, thin-cut ribeye steak, grilled and topped with sautéed onions, bell peppers, and tomatoes, served with a chicken enchilada, refried beans, and pico de gallo on tortilla.

4882 Utica Ridge Rd., Davenport, IA, 563-359-3660
5304 Avenue of the Cities, Moline, IL, 309-757-1505
3939 16th St., Moline, IL, 309-757-7134
losagavesmexicangrill.net

TIP
Beyond Los Agaves, the multitude of high-quality Mexican in the area includes Azteca, La Rancherita, Adolph's, Los Portales, Verde, D'Lua, Rudy's Tacos, Old Mexico, Tacobar, Los Amigos, El Patron, and Coya's Cafe.

FLY HIGH WITH HISTORY
AT THE CRANE & PELICAN CAFE

Since 2009, the Crane & Pelican has served classy comfort food in an elegant historic mansion overlooking the Mississippi River. The Dawley House was built in 1851 and is listed on the National Register of Historic Places. Daniel and Sabina Dawley raised nine children in the home, and they were prominent members of early LeClaire. The lovely restaurant prides itself on making food from scratch and lovingly taking care of every detail of the dining experience. That care and attention shows. They also host private events and offer live jazz on most Thursday and Friday nights (including on the lawn in the warmer months).

127 2nd St. S, LeClaire, IA, 563-289-8774
craneandpelican.com

TIP
Try a local cocktail called "The Big LeClaireski," made with River Pilot Vodka, Kahlua, Butterscotch Schnapps, and Iowish Cream served on the rocks.

MORE EXCELLENT LECLAIRE EATERIES

The Faithful Pilot
One of the QC's best restaurants, they offer fine
dining and extraordinary wine and spirits in an
intimate setting along the Mississippi River.
117 N Cody Rd., 563-289-4156
faithfulpilot.com

Steventon's
Sitting up on a bluff in LeClaire here allows
an exceptional view of the mighty Mississippi.
Steventon's also offers a large patio and a cozy firepit,
and its delectable menu features several fiery
dishes flambéed tableside.
1399 Eagle Ridge Rd., 563-289-3600
steventons.com

Blue Iguana
This newer, hip eatery is a truly authentic, fresh
Mexican cantina. Its fun atmosphere features
mouthwatering guacamole, tasty tacos, fajitas,
and burritos; ice cold, refreshing margaritas;
and much more.
201 N Cody Rd., 563-729-1015
the-blueiguana.com

BASK IN GLORY
AT HOTEL BLACKHAWK'S BIX BISTRO

Even if you don't stay there overnight, downtown Davenport's Hotel Blackhawk is a must-see destination. Built in 1915, this 11-story icon was badly deteriorating before a loving, meticulous $46-million renovation and expansion. It reopened in 2010 with a sumptuous two-story lobby (the couches are so comfy!) and a spectacular stained-glass skylight. The hotel has hosted many celebrities over the years, including Barack Obama, Cary Grant, plus other entertainers, legendary athletes, and Quad Cities's business leaders who live in its luxury apartments. The first floor features the contemporary, sleek Bix Bistro, offering great food prepared with local and fresh ingredients. Named for perhaps Davenport's most famous son, the Bix offers a large selection of beer, wine, and spirits.

200 E 3rd St., Davenport, IA, 855-958-0973
hotelblackhawk.com

TIP

On the hotel's lower level is the equally stylish Blackhawk Bowl, featuring a fully stocked bar with extensive martini list as well as tasty, "beyond traditional" bowling alley eats, and the first level includes the Rise Neighborhood Café.

START A GLOBAL GASTRONOMIC TRIP
AT EXOTIC THAI OR TANTRA

The QC boasts a staggering variety of international restaurants, and just choosing among Thai places is a gourmand's dream. My favorites are along Davenport's busy 53rd Street corridor—Exotic Thai and Tantra. Both present delicious dishes with great attention to detail and flavor. Exotic Thai features a tantalizingly titled "Crying Tiger," a New York strip lightly marinated and grilled to perfection, with a sauce "spicy enough to make a tiger cry." I love the "Madam Curry" entrées, especially Kang Dang, a spicy red curry with coconut milk, bamboo shoots, and bell peppers. Tantra Asian Bistro is large, relaxing, and upscale; includes outdoor patio seating; and boasts a tremendously varied menu.

Exotic Thai
2303 E 53rd St., Davenport, IA
563-344-0909
exoticthaiqc.com

Tantra Asian Bistro
589 E 53rd St., Davenport, IA
563-445-8898
tantramenu.com

TIP
Try these other QC Thai standouts: Sriracha Thai Oyster Bar and LemonGrass in Moline, Miss Phay Cafe in Davenport, Soi 2 in Rock Island, and Soi 3 in Davenport.

AMONG CULINARY GLOBETROTTING TRAVELS, SAMPLE THESE OUTSTANDING FOREIGN FLAVORS

Trattoria Tiramisu (Italian)
1804 State St., Bettendorf, IA, 563-355-0749
trattoria-tiramisu.business.site

Uncle Pete's (Greek)
3629 Avenue of the Cities, Moline, IL, 309-762-6877
unclepetesgyros.com

Mantra (Indian)
220 N Harrison St., Davenport, IA, 563-424-5500
mantraqc.com

Bier Stube (German)
415 15th St., Moline, IL, 309-797-3049
1001 Canal Shore Dr. SW, LeClaire, IA, 563-289-2121
bier-stube.com

Red Lantern (Chinese)
4009 E 53rd St., Davenport, IA, 563-355-7970
redlanternfineia.com

Hi Ho Mongolian Grill (Mongolian)
901 E Kimberly Rd., Davenport, IA, 563-445-0800

Le Mekong (Vietnamese)
1606 5th Ave., Moline, IL, 309-797-8660
lemekongqca.com

Red Ginger Sushi Grill & Bar (Japanese)
793 Middle Rd., Bettendorf, IA, 563-355-4898
redgingeria.com

Zeke's Island Cafe (Jamaican)
131 W 2nd St., Davenport, IA, (inside RME) 563-499-0550

Zeke's Island Express (Jamaican)
842 Middle Rd., Bettendorf, IA

Zeke's Tropical Tacos (Jamaican)
5039 Competition Dr., Bettendorf, IA (at Bettplex)
zekesrestaurants.com

Pee Wee's Restaurant (Cajun/Creole Soul Food)
2035 Martin Luther King Dr., Rock Island, IL
309-283-7930
facebook.com/peeweesrestaurantri

Hemispheres Bistro (International)
2504 E 53rd Ave., Bettendorf, IA, 563-332-2370
hemispheresbistro.com

Food Affair Bistro (International)
1015 Utica Ridge Ct., Bettendorf, IA, 563-214-0610
foodaffairbistro.com

Photo courtesy of Joseph Maciejko

MUSIC
AND ENTERTAINMENT

FIND YOUR FAVORITE EVENT
AT THE TAXSLAYER CENTER

Like many arenas and stadiums nationwide, the TaxSlayer Center in Moline has undergone name changes since it opened in 1993, signaling a major revitalization of downtown Moline and the QC area overall. The 11,000-seat arena along the shore of the Mississippi began life as The MARK of the Quad Cities (which many here still call it), opening with two nights of Neil Diamond. Including a conference room and meeting space, the TaxSlayer (since 2017 and before that the iWireless Center since 2007) has hosted a staggering number of big concert tours, such as Frank Sinatra, Prince, David Bowie, Keith Urban, James Taylor, Barry Manilow, the Eagles, and Paul McCartney. Also headlining here are Disney on Ice shows, monster truck shows, and rodeos. This is also the home for the QC's minor-league football and hockey teams—the Quad City Steamwheelers and Quad City Storm, respectively.

1201 River Dr., Moline, IL, 309-764-2001
taxslayercenter.com

ENJOY A CONCERT, SHOW, AND MORE
AT THE ADLER THEATRE/RIVERCENTER

Connected physically and by one address in downtown Davenport, the historic Adler Theatre and later add-on convention center are together a longtime focal point for culture, special events, conferences, and many private receptions in the QC. The sumptuous 2,400-seat Adler began life in 1931 as a grand movie palace, the RKO Orpheum. Since 1986, it's been home to the Quad City Symphony Orchestra and many big-name touring artists, including Broadway productions, as well as the cherished annual *Nutcracker* from Ballet Quad Cities. The RiverCenter began in 1983, and has been enlarged and renovated over the years. With two buildings (on either side of East 3rd Street), the center boasts 100,000 square feet of flexible space, with two column-free exhibit halls, hosting many meetings, conventions, trade shows, athletic events, and other special events and banquets.

136 E 3rd St., Davenport, IA, 563-326-8500
adlertheatre.com
riverctr.com

MILK THE STAGE
AT TWO BARN THEATRES:
PLAYCRAFTERS AND RICHMOND HILL

Two unique, intimate theaters are housed in former dairy barns. The first, Playcrafters in Moline, is one of the oldest theater companies in the region, founded in 1929. It took up residence in a 1914 barn in 1960. Playcrafters has made many renovations in the decades since, and features a thrust stage with seating on three sides. Twenty-two miles east, in Geneseo, is the bucolic and even cozier Richmond Hill Barn Theatre. This dates from 1968, and like Playcrafters, the theater is on the second floor of the old dairy barn. Richmond Hill seats 160 per performance in a rare and unique in-the-round environment beneath the original, rustic timbers. Both venues typically do straight plays—dramas, comedies, and mysteries, and Playcrafters extends to an occasional musical.

Playcrafters
4950 35th Ave., Moline, IL, 309-762-0330
playcrafters.com

Richmond Hill
Richmond Hill Park, Geneseo, IL, 309-944-2244
rhplayers.com

TIP

In 2017, the Moline theater started a Barn Owl series that tackles edgier, more contemporary fare.

TAKE A CULTURAL RIDE
AT THE RIVER MUSIC EXPERIENCE

The River Music Experience—RME for short—is not only smack-dab in the middle of downtown Davenport, it's often at the center of the QC's cultural life. It gave bustling new life to the 1892 Redstone building. While RME began as a museum devoted to music influenced by the Mississippi River, it's become a multi-faceted community arts group that finds ways to present music inside and far outside its walls. The second-floor Redstone Room is one of the best places to hear live music and its outdoor courtyard hosts a summer Live@Five free Friday series. What's more, the joint offers many educational programs to help change lives.

129 Main St., Davenport, IA, 563-326-1333
rivermusicexperience.org

TIP

Be sure to take in the display outside the Redstone Room on the late Ellis Kell (one of RME's most influential leaders), and on the Main Street side, admire a phenomenal mural that pays tribute to the six partner organizations of the QC Cultural Trust, of which RME is one.

GET SWEPT UP IN BEAUTY
AT BALLET QUAD CITIES

A Ballet Quad Cities performance is virtually guaranteed to be elegant, energetic, and exquisitely beautiful, at varied venues throughout the area. The only professional dance company between Chicago and Kansas City, it provides creative classical and contemporary dance to the entire community through exceptional, meticulous, and emotional performances; enlightening lecture-demonstrations; and educational outreach programs for people of all ages. The ballet's outreach includes DREAMS Achieved Through Dance, Dance Me a Story, Exploring Literature through Ballet, and the Ugly Duckling Bullying Prevention Program, giving back to thousands of elementary school students in the region.

613 17th St., Rock Island, IL, 309-786-3779
balletquadcities.com

LISTEN TO A CLASSIC
FROM THE QUAD CITY SYMPHONY

A cultural treasure in the area, the Quad City Symphony Orchestra, or QCSO, is among the 20 longest continuously operating professional orchestras in the nation, since its 1916 debut. Led by the unpretentious, articulate maestro, Mark Russell Smith, the orchestra consistently delivers concerts of high quality, passion, and commitment, rivaling those of much larger cities. Each season, the QCSO performs approximately 20 times, presenting six Masterworks concerts, three Pops series concerts including the Quad City Bank & Trust Riverfront Pops, Films in Concert, and special events. In addition, the Up Close Series, led by concertmaster Naha Greenholtz, presents chamber music ensembles in an intimate setting that features select members of the QCSO and visiting artists from across the nation. The orchestra also has dedicated youth ensembles (serving over 270 students a year), strong educational outreach, and community partnerships.

327 Brady St., Davenport, IA, 563-322-0931
qcso.org

GET UP CLOSE AND PERSONAL
WITH BLACK BOX THEATRE

Since transforming a former retail space in downtown Moline into a magically intimate, literal black-box theater (opening in January 2017), this 60-seat venue has been home to a dazzling variety of thoughtful, enormously entertaining productions. Small musicals, dramas, comedies, radio plays, and improv comedy all have found a welcoming space and appreciative audiences. Co-founded by the tireless, supportive Lora Adams and David Miller (who often have directed their shows), the Black Box has given me some unforgettable times both on and off stage, including music directing *The Last Five Years* and performing as John Hinckley in *Assassins*. The audience proximity to performers offers electrifying, magical moments in theater.

1623 5th Ave., Moline, IL, 563-284-2350
theblackboxtheatre.com

BASK IN
THE BEST OF BROADWAY
WITH THE QUAD CITY MUSIC GUILD

Since the beloved Quad City Music Guild was launched with an operetta in 1949 in a 1903 Chautauqua pavilion, much has changed to update and expand the theater in Moline's beautiful Prospect Park. What hasn't changed is the nonprofit's commitment to presenting the best of Broadway musicals, five per season, completely due to the hard work of volunteers, including directing, acting, choreography, orchestra, lighting, sound, set construction, and concessions. Guild workers range from senior citizens to grade-school youngsters, contributing countless hours of community involvement to the Guild. The terrific talents at Guild include a costume shop that rents to area schools and other theaters, a youth chorus, and scholarships for the community. In 2015, the theater welcomed its 750,000th patron.

1584 34th Ave., Moline, IL, 309-762-6610
qcmusicguild.com

PRAISE A HIGHER POWER
AT THE SPOTLIGHT THEATRE

You could say attending the Spotlight Theatre and Event Center is a religious experience. After all, the family-run venue (including a 600-seat theater with a stunning, soaring proscenium arch) is in an imposing three-story former Scottish Rite Cathedral, built in 1930. Since formally opening in 2018 with a perfect melding of setting and show (*The Hunchback of Notre Dame*), the Spotlight stages a wide variety of musicals, improv shows, and other entertainment. It offers children's programming, hosts weddings and receptions, and is home to the swanky Blueprint Bar + Lounge, which has hosted a jazz lounge series.

1800 7th Ave., Moline, IL, 309-912-7647
thespotlighttheatreqc.com

TIP
Also check out The Market: A Journey to Joy in the building, which boasts locally produced, handcrafted merchandise, ranging from home décor and women's clothing to bath and body products, kitchenware, plants, flowers, food, and almost everything in between. They also have a new location at 430 North Cody Road, LeClaire, Iowa.

SAMPLE A VARIETY OF ENTERTAINMENT
AT THE RUST BELT

Echoing the QC's history as a manufacturing capital in the Midwest, the Rust Belt is an exciting 4,000-capacity standing-room concert venue that transformed a former industrial plant. Its perfect location next to the river and the beautiful Bend development (including a stunning, sleek Hyatt hotel and casual, fresh Combine restaurant) led to the further transformation of neighboring brick buildings. The Rust Belt has hosted a variety of rock, country, and hip-hop shows, and has a full-service bar, but doesn't sell food in the music hall.

533 12th Ave., East Moline, IL
therustbeltqc.com

TIP

You don't have to look far to serve that appetite, since the complex boasts Jennie's Boxcar (a street taco restaurant that also honors the area's Mexican immigrant heritage); Sweet Arnie's (with some of the best BBQ in town), and Iron + Grain Coffee House. The excellent craft brewery Midwest Ale Works is also right here.

SOAR
AT THE NEW MOCKINGBIRD ON MAIN

Local actors Tristan Tapscott and Savannah Bay Strandin love theater, each other, and *To Kill a Mockingbird* so in early 2021 they poured their hearts, souls, and savings into creating a unique theater in downtown Davenport, Mockingbird on Main. Formerly occupied by the bridal shop and boutique Blush, the sophisticated space (with some gorgeous chandeliers left from the shop) was renovated into an intimate cabaret to seat 40 at tables with a small 12-foot-by-8-foot stage. The owners encourage any performers and writers in the area to bring their creativity and vision to the Mockingbird, and it's given birth to some fantastic flights of fancy in its short, varied life so far.

320 N Main St., Davenport, IA, 309-781-5972
themockingbirdonmain.com

PARK YOURSELF IN ROCK ISLAND
FOR THE GENESIUS GUILD

Each summer, Lincoln Park in Rock Island (near Augustana's campus) is home to the Genesius Guild, which provides a unique theater experience to audiences of all ages. The performances are staged on Saturdays and Sundays outdoors between a half-circle of Greek columns and an elegant Bedford stone building. This natural setting beneath the trees and stars provides the perfect atmosphere for staging classic Greek and Shakespearean plays. Since 1956, the Genesius Guild has remained focused on staging ancient Greek and Shakespearean comedies and tragedies, as well as Greek comedies carefully rewritten to maintain the flavor of the original while updating the jokes to be relevant in today's society. Ballet Quad Cities usually starts the summer season, and Lincoln Park also hosts a free summer concert series during the week.

1120 40th St., Rock Island, IL, 309-794-8900
genesius.org

BECOME A KID AGAIN
AT DAVENPORT JUNIOR THEATRE

Founded in 1951, Davenport Junior Theatre is the second-oldest children's theater in the nation, and it promises "theatre for kids, by kids." That means for their mainstage productions, the students work alongside professional artists to put together each production. Junior Theatre has been giving area youth the opportunity to learn to speak clearly, confidently, and creatively in any social setting since 1976. It offers classes in acting, musical theater, technical theater, and dance plus summer camps. Its theater home (a former chapel that retains its stained-glass windows) has been renovated many times over the years.

2822 Eastern Ave., Davenport, IA
davenportjuniortheatre.org
bucktownreview.com

TIP

Davenport Junior Theatre has also served as home for the monthly variety show *The Bucktown Revue* for several years. That *Prairie Home Companion*-style show focuses on folk, bluegrass, and Americana, and is held on the third Friday of the month from September to May.

HANG OUT WITH COOL CUISINE, MUSIC, AND FILMS
AT ROZZ-TOX

It's almost impossible to classify Rozz-Tox in Rock Island, which has been an epicenter of cool since 2011. The diverse place (which includes a side patio and back garden) does a pretty good job describing itself—"a listening bar, café, brasserie, zakka, performance venue, gallery, culture cell, guesthouse, library, cinema, club; a virus whose ultimate goal is to constantly mutate to avoid becoming part of mainstream culture." The wide-ranging menu (including bao, Japanese curry, beer, wine, coffee, and tea) reflects the Asian background of owner Benjamin Fawks, who lived in South China before returning to his hometown. In recent years, other Rozz-Tox locations have opened in China. In Rock Island, every event has a different vibe—from spoken word to German film to the next band you should know. Rozz-Tox proudly marches to its own relaxed, adventurous, wonderful drummer.

2108 3rd Ave., Rock Island, IL, 309-200-0978
rozztox.com

FEAST ON DINNER AND A SHOW
AT CIRCA '21

Circa '21 Dinner Playhouse is not just rare in the QC, but across the country. Dinner theaters have dwindled over decades, and that makes the downtown Rock Island showplace special, for several reasons. Named for its original use as a 1921 movie palace, Denny Hitchcock reopened Circa in 1977 as a 330-seat dinner theater. It's specialized in musicals, as well as comedies and dramas. One unique feature is the performing wait staff, The Bootleggers. The Circa staff is beloved for being super friendly, and you feel like family when you're there. The Bootleggers do a short pre-show, with songs and dance, and the whole package of food, drink, and entertainment is delicious. Circa's mainstage hosts many children's shows and concerts of tribute acts.

1828 3rd Ave., Rock Island, IL, 309-786-7733, ext. 2
circa21.com

TIP

Next door, Circa runs The Speakeasy, a 125-seat venue that has a lineup of more adult fare, including burlesque, drag shows, big bands, and stand-up comedy.

TRY YOUR LUCK
AT CASINOS—BALLY'S, THE ISLE, AND RHYTHM CITY

The QC has been home to casinos since 1991, when the first modern riverboat casinos in the nation opened on the Mississippi River in Iowa. Gaming has taken many twists and turns since, including moving off the river years ago. The Isle Casino Hotel in Bettendorf is the only one next to the river—with nearly 1,000 slot machines and favorite table games, the largest hotel in Iowa (500+ rooms and suites), and three restaurants. Bally's Quad Cities in Rock Island has more than 850 slots and 24 table games, as well as a live poker room, high-limit slot area, and VIP lounge. Amenities include a 205-room hotel, an events center with meeting rooms for up to 500 people, and four restaurants. Rhythm City Casino Resort in north Davenport is the newest (from 2016), boasting 1,000 slot machines, 25 table games, the Elite Sports Book, a hotel, three restaurants, a full-service spa, and an event center.

Bally's Quad Cities Casino & Hotel
777 Bally Blvd., Rock Island, IL
ballys.com/quad-cities

Isle Casino Hotel Bettendorf
1777 Isle Pkwy., Bettendorf, IA, 563-441-7000
islebettendorf.com

Rhythm City Casino Resort
7077 Elmore Ave., Davenport, IA, 563-328-8000
rhythmcitycasino.com

HAVE MORE THAN A FAIR TIME
AT THE MISSISSIPPI VALLEY FAIRGROUNDS

The Mississippi Valley Fairgrounds in west Davenport has been a center for fun and education since 1920. In addition to its summertime pinnacle event—the six-day Mississippi Valley Fair, featuring carnival rides, food, 4-H competitions, and top-tier musical acts—the fairgrounds host countless other year-round events and parties in its state-of-the-art facilities. These include car and motorcycle shows, concerts, dirt track racing, weddings, flea markets, gun shows, and political events. It added the 30,000-square-foot Fair Center in 2011 and the 20,000-square-foot Iowa Building in 2014. The fairgrounds' mission is to offer family-oriented programs that are innovative, entertaining, educational, rural and urban, competitive, and fun for all ages.

2815 W Locust St., Davenport, IA, 563-326-5338
mvfair.com

FIND YOUR MUSIC PASSION
AT THE RACCOON MOTEL
AND CODFISH HOLLOW

Two well-known, unique live music venues are 40 miles apart, worth checking out, and both booked with events by Daytrotter co-founder and music impresario Sean Moeller. For years, he's had his finger on the pulse of hot rising artists in a wide range of genres. The current Raccoon Motel in downtown Davenport is not an actual motel, but is the second version after its first iteration in another downtown bar (2017–19). The current live-music venue and bar have a capacity of about 200, twice the size of the old place. About 40 miles north, outside Maquoketa, Moeller since 2009 has led booking acts at the Codfish Hollow barn. With live music from April through October, it's well worth the jaunt. When it is lit up at night and surrounded by food and drink vendors, it's magical.

The Raccoon Motel
315 E 2nd St., Davenport, IA
theraccoonmotel.com

Codfish Hollow
5013 288th Ave., Maquoketa, IA
codfishhollowbarnstormers.com

TOAST TO LIVE MUSIC HISTORY
AT RIBCO

A destination for great food, beer, and live music is Rock Island Brewing Company. Founded in 1979 in a former nightclub and named for one of the QC's oldest breweries, RIBCO has served up a variety of brews and bands for generations, including many big names who stopped here on their way up such as Tracy Chapman and Barenaked Ladies. The popular lunch spot and bar's success can be attributed to its niche in emphasizing quality music. It's not a sports bar with TVs everywhere, and it's not a bar with a band stuck in the corner. Live music has been front and center for years. The plaza in downtown Rock Island hosts outdoor shows and festivals, including Ya Maka My Weekend.

1815 2nd Ave., Rock Island, IL
ribco.com

TIP

RIBCO's neighbor, Daiquiri Factory (whose owner, Kyle Peters, books for the Rust Belt), also is a frequent host of energetic, hopping live shows. 1809 2nd Ave., Rock Island, IL, daiquirifactory.com

MAKE A BEELINE FOR BIX
AT HIS JAZZ FEST AND MUSEUM

The QC in early August is a must, since that's when we honor Davenport's most famous son, Leon "Bix" Beiderbecke (1903–1931), the legendary jazz cornetist, pianist, and composer. The Bix Beiderbecke Memorial Jazz Festival had its 50th anniversary in 2021. One of the longest continuously operating jazz fests in the nation, it persistently and beautifully keeps the classic, exuberant music of the '20s and '30s alive. Be sure to get to know Bix personally and musically in the free Bix Museum at River Music Experience, which opened in 2017. Treasured recordings (which play in the museum) keep alive his unique tone, style, lyrical phrasing, and heart-stopping improvisations. The illuminating museum is filled with photos, videos, recordings, instruments, and other artifacts.

The Bix Beiderbecke Memorial Jazz Festival
Davenport, IA, 563-324-7170
bixsociety.org

Bix Museum
2nd and Main streets, Lower Level, Davenport, IA, 701-318-9288
bixmuseum.org

TIP
The Beiderbecke gravesite is at Oakdale Memorial Gardens and his boyhood home can be found at 1934 Grand Avenue, Davenport, Iowa.

Photo courtesy of Modern Woodmen Park

SPORTS
AND RECREATION

GET ON THE BEATEN PATH
WITH NATIONAL TRAILS

Quad Cities is unique as the nexus for the nationwide American
Discovery Trail (ADT) and Mississippi River Trail (MRT). The
ADT passes through the area on its journey from the Pacific
to the Atlantic coasts, entering in the east along the Hennepin
Parkway State Trail, through Colona, Illinois, crossing the
Rock River along Illinois 84, and turning north to meet the
Great River Trail (GRT) along the Mississippi. Following the
GRT in Illinois, trail enthusiasts will see sweeping views of the
Mississippi across to the Iowa shoreline. The ADT continues
on the Mississippi River Trail (MRT) west through Davenport,
across Credit Island, and along the river. Running over 60 miles
from Rock Island to Savanna, Illinois, the QC portion of the
MRT is a multipurpose trail for all ages and abilities. The trail
connects to many neighborhoods, shopping districts, and parks
and recreation areas. Picturesque riverfront vistas are abundant
all along the trail in Illinois and along the MRT in Iowa.

qctrails.org/trails

TEE UP A GOOD TIME
AT TPC DEERE RUN

One of Quad Cities's prettiest places is the TPC Deere Run golf course, on the site of a former Arabian horse farm. D. A. Weibring preserved the rolling landscape along the Rock River to create a championship course framed by oak trees and accented by small ponds and deep ravines. This course is best known as home of the summertime John Deere Classic, one of the major success stories on the PGA Tour. Since the early '70s, the tournament has withstood changes in location and title sponsors, and has thrived as a community-based, charity-oriented tournament. It consistently ranks as #1 on the Tour in per-capita giving. The JDC provides annual financial contributions to local charities and promotes volunteerism. The course has been featured as one of America's 100 Greatest Public Golf Courses by *Golf Digest*.

3100 Heather Knoll, Silvis, IL, 309-796-6000
tpc.com/deererun

FIND LOTS TO DO AND SEE
ON PICTURESQUE CREDIT ISLAND

Credit Island in southwest Davenport is a 450-acre park and the site of a battle during the War of 1812. The island got its name from its use as a fur trading post. Park amenities include two baseball diamonds, a basketball court, a boat ramp, the renovated Credit Island Lodge, an 18-hole disc golf course, multiple historic areas, horseshoe pits, nature trails, two playgrounds, four reservable shelters, and tennis courts. Motorists can access the island's walking paths and biking trails via West River Drive and turning south onto Credit Island Road to access parking and amenities. Pedestrians and cyclists can get on the island via a pedestrian bridge on the southern tip of the island crossing Concord Street.

2301 W River Dr., Davenport, IA, 563-328-7275
qctrails.org/trails/trail/credit-island-park-walking-path

TIP
Check out the island's sculptures, depicting figures in the painting *Sunday Afternoon on the Island of La Grande Jatte* by Georges Seurat. Installed in 1998, this interpretation of the painting was created by artist Ted McElhiney and sculptor Thom Gleich.

CROSS FOUR CITIES AND TWO STATES
IN QUAD CITIES MARATHON

Since 1998, the TBK Quad Cities Marathon has become a Midwest favorite. Touching four cities and spanning two states, it attracts runners from all over and boasts a weekend of activities up until the main event on the fourth Sunday in September. The scenic 26.2-mile run starts and ends in downtown Moline. The views are amazing, the Midwestern charm is present, and the course is fairly fast. It's a Boston Marathon qualifier, covering five races (including a half-marathon, a 5K, one-mile race, and kids' micro-marathon), four cities, three bridges, two states, and one island, all along the mighty Mississippi. Hundreds of volunteers make sure that the course is ready, and spectators are a vital part of the marathon as everyone is encouraged to line the course. Part of the proceeds go to buy running shoes for Quad Cities youth and to support the QC Prostate Cancer Initiative.

qcmarathon.org

BANK ON FINDING IT ALL
AT THE TBK BANK SPORTS COMPLEX

The TBK Bank Sports Complex is virtually a small, busy city unto itself. The sprawling sports and entertainment center alone includes a 273,000-square-foot facility with an indoor multipurpose turf field, eight basketball/volleyball courts, a training area, a fitness center, physical therapy space, 32 bowling lanes, 65 arcade games, two-story laser tag, escape rooms, a virtual reality attraction, a multi-sport simulator, a sports bar and restaurant, banquet and meeting space, outdoor soccer fields, baseball fields, sand volleyball courts, and over 1,500 parking spaces. The complex features a TBK Bank Sports Academy and is home to tournaments throughout the Midwest.

4850 Competition Dr., Bettendorf, IA, 563-723-7529 (sports)
563-447-2695 (entertainment)
tbkbanksportscomplex.com

TIP

The variety of amenities that surround the complex include an upscale Cambria hotel and restaurants and bars specializing in health food, Mexican, pizza, mac and cheese, craft beer, donuts, tacos, coffee, and cookies. Conveniently, if you overdo it with Cheesy Cow or Hurts Donuts, there are lots of exercise options right next door.

MORE TBK-SPONSORED COOLNESS

New Entertainment Venue Opening in 2023

Across the street from the sprawling Bettendorf complex by fall 2023 will be a new 70,000-square-foot golf entertainment venue, with 60+ climate-controlled outdoor hitting bays, menu items, top-shelf drinks, music, and year-round entertainment. Many high-definition TVs will be located throughout the facility with one oversized 4K LED TV—estimated to be the largest (indoor) TV in the state of Iowa—in the main bar area. Year-round programming will include events for kids and families, golf tournaments, social leagues, corporate events, showers and graduation parties, concerts, charity events, and more. The venue will also feature a state-of-the-art video gaming space, which will include an immersive virtual reality platform, escape rooms, multi-sport simulators with several multi-sport (baseball, softball, and soccer) turf fields outside, which will be managed by TBK Bank Sports Complex.

TAKE A WALK OR BIKE
ACROSS THE NEW I-74 BRIDGE

One of the most exciting developments in recent QC history was the long-awaited December 2021 completion of the $1.2-billion I-74 Bridge, connecting Moline and Bettendorf. Replacing the landmark twin suspension two-lane bridges (originally built in 1935 and 1959), the new white-arched bridge has four lanes of traffic in each direction. The stunning bridge—illuminated at night with a varying number of LED lights—includes a 14-foot-wide bike and pedestrian path with a scenic overlook and connections to existing paths in Bettendorf and Moline. The long-planned project (under construction four and a half years) was the largest in Iowa state history.

i74riverbridge.com

TIP

On the Iowa side, there will be a tinted-glass, eight-story elevator that will sit against the west side of the bridge on the newly landscaped Bettendorf riverfront. The structure will provide pedestrians and bicyclists easy access to the 14-foot-wide concrete trail on the Illinois-bound side of the bridge.

TRAVERSE
A HEAVENLY TRAIL
ALONG THE HENNEPIN CANAL

A great day trip is tracking the Hennepin Canal State Trail in Illinois, where you can spend a day picknicking, hiking, biking, and fishing. There are several picnic tables along the 104-mile park spanning five Illinois counties (Rock Island, Bureau, Henry, Lee, and Whiteside). Built from 1892 to 1907, the Hennepin Canal played an important role in US history and is on the National Register of Historic Places. Connecting the Illinois River to the Rock River, parts of the trails are open to horseback riding and snowmobile riding in season. The canal is open for boating and canoeing, but locks are not operational. Campgrounds and day-use areas are located all along the canal.

illinois.gov/dnr/parks/pages/hennepincanal.aspx

TIP
Before exploring, you should check the Visitor Center near Sheffield where there are displays illustrating the canal's past as well as natural features.

SLIDE INTO FAMILY FUN
AT SNOWSTAR

Snowstar is the QC's only outdoor winter fun park offering alpine skiing, freestyle terrain park, and trained and certified instruction for both alpine skiing and snowboarding. It also offers the region's only snow-tubing hill with 11 groomed lanes, a warming hut, a portable bathroom, and snacks and beverages. Snowstar provides indoor seating in the Lunar Lodge with two fireplaces. Here a full line of prepared food and beverages is available for purchase. There is also a full-service pub and Internet lounge, Rex's Rendezvous. You can beat the winter blues by coming out to Snowstar typically from December through March. The sports area is open year-round, offering zip-line tours, the area's only champion-level disc golf course, paintball, event rentals, four unique food and beverage options, and more. Many improvements were made in 2021, including online reservations, a ticket-window shed and snack trailer, an expanded warming hut, new lighting and signage, and cool galaxy tubing after dark.

9500 126th St. W, Andalusia, IL, 800-383-4002
skisnowstar.com

PARK YOURSELF FOR EXERCISE OR A MEAL
ON THE BEN BUTTERWORTH PARKWAY

One of the best riverfront trails is the 2.2-mile Ben Butterworth Parkway, along the Moline shoreline, just east of downtown to the city's edge. The parkway features three playgrounds, a marina, two boat launches, gardens, two picnic shelters, benches, restrooms, a fishing pier (ADA), fitness equipment, a memorial patio, and bike racks. Try the Captain's Table, which has a 60-year history of providing steak and seafood on the Mississippi River. After a 2018 fire, the new building and new commercially built marina include many elements from the old, including a Captain's Table room, porthole windows, and fish-tank booths. The new place also includes excellent seating inside and outside. With a new deck and the main level elevated over five feet from ground level, there's not a bad seat in the house.

22nd–55th Streets along River Dr., Moline, IL

Captain's Table
4801 River Dr., Moline, IL
thecaptainstablemoline.com

THRILL TO HOCKEY
WITH THE QUAD CITY STORM

Two years after the Moline arena opened, the area's first minor-league hockey team took the QC by storm, and the sport has been popular here ever since. The Quad City Mallards (1995–2007 and 2009–2018) won seven league championships, and since 2018, the Storm has skated on arena ice. Owner John Dawson is a Rock Island native and US Air Force veteran who appropriately plays hockey in his free time. The Storm logo is an angry tornado wielding a lightning-bolt hockey stick, but its cuddly team mascot is Radar the Fox. The Storm not only connects with fans in the arena (in many promotions), from October to early May, but works to connect to the community by partnering with many local organizations.

TaxSlayer Center
1201 River Dr., Moline, IL, 309-277-1343
quadcitystorm.com

LOOK FOR INDOOR SPIKES
WITH THE QC STEAMWHEELERS

For over 20 years, the TaxSlayer Center has hosted arena football, with the Quad City Steamwheelers, first in the AF2 league from 2000 to 2009 where they won the first two league championships. The game (invented and patented in the 1980s) is played indoors on a smaller field than American football—50 yards long instead of 100—to fit in the same surface area as a standard North American ice hockey rink. This results in a faster and higher-scoring game that can be played on the floors of indoor arenas (usually from March to July), and arena football teams sport eight players at a time (unlike the NFL's 11). The current Steamwheelers played their first season as part of the Champions Indoor Football but joined the Indoor Football League prior to their second season.

Quad City Steamwheelers
1201 River Dr., Moline, IL, 563-888-1551
steamwheelersfootball.com

HEAR THE BATS CRACK
AT MODERN WOODMEN PARK

One of the best views in the QC is the Centennial Bridge from the third-base side of Modern Woodmen Park, or better, from atop its Ferris wheel during a game of minor-league baseball's River Bandits, an affiliate of the Kansas City Royals. Since 1987, St. Ambrose University has also played its home baseball games there. Located on the banks of the Mississippi, in the 4,000-seat stadium, home-run balls to right field often land in the river. First opened in 1931 as Municipal Stadium, in 1971 it was renamed John O'Donnell Stadium for a longtime sports editor, then Modern Woodmen Park in 2007 after Rock Island-based Modern Woodmen of America purchased naming rights. O'Donnell's name remains on the ballpark's press box. There's family fun to be had around the stadium beyond the game.

209 S Gaines St., Davenport, IA, 563-324-3000
milb.com/quad-cities

TIP
Besides the 110-foot-tall Ferris wheel, there's a carousel, a kids roller-coaster, bounce houses, and other rides.

ENJOY THE GREAT OUTDOORS
AT LOUD THUNDER AND ILLINIWEK

Two areas well worth seeing are Illiniwek and Loud Thunder Forest Preserve. Illiniwek, adjoining the east side of Hampton, Illinois, along Route 84, contains 198 acres. The forest-preserve setting on the Mississippi River is ideally situated for recreation both on land and in the water. Facilities available at the park include camping areas, 60 pads with water and electric hookups, shower houses, a boat-launch ramp, hiking trails, a picnic shelter, and a wooded bluff picnic area overlooking the river. Loud Thunder—in Illinois City, off Highway 92—has 1,480 acres that are home to picnic shelters, campgrounds, trails, biking paths, two playgrounds, and Lake George. You can also rent a kayak, canoe, Jon Boat, two-person pontoon boat, or even a Party Barge to get out on the lake.

ricfpd.org

ADMIRE A UNIQUE PARK
AT SYLVAN ISLAND

Less than a mile from downtown Moline, you can get away from it all at peaceful, picturesque Sylvan Island, three-quarters of a mile west of the John Deere Commons. The 37-acre island was once home to a steel mill, of which remnants can still be seen—concrete loading docks and building foundations, railroad tracks, rebar, and loose rock. It's a perfect, convenient refuge, and you'll often have the island to yourself. There is a 1.2-mile network of multi-use trails across from Moline's Sylvan Island Gateway Park (on the mainland). The trails are great for fishing, hiking, and mountain biking and the island amenities include fishing, benches and picnic tables, an informational kiosk, a water fountain, and a canoe/kayak portage.

1st Avenue and 2nd Street, Moline, IL
moline.il.us/1167/sylvan-island

ENJOY WATER
AT SCHWIEBERT RIVERFRONT PARK

The beautiful and popular Schwiebert Riverfront Park is my favorite Quad Cities park, named after my favorite QC mayor. In downtown Rock Island, along the river between 17th and 20th Streets, the park was created in 2010 on the former site of the Rock Island Armory and Casino Rock Island. It is named for former Mayor Mark Schwiebert (1989–2009), an articulate, passionate public servant, for his tireless efforts to promote public use of the riverfront. In addition to its spectacular views of the Mississippi and downtown Davenport, the gorgeous park features sculptures, an innovative digital playground, fountains, water sprays, a great lawn, observation shelter, a promenade, a 3,000-square-foot stage, restrooms, a triangle lawn, an urban concrete beach, a trail, and a boat dock. Live concerts are featured throughout the summer, and the park is also an area favorite for weddings, receptions, and special events. Whenever you're at Schwiebert Park, it's special.

18th Street and the Mississippi River, Rock Island, IL, 309-732-7275
rigov.org/facilities/facility/details/34

JOIN RUNNERS FROM AROUND THE WORLD
AT BIX 7

Runners from around the world converge on Davenport in late July every year for the Quad-City Times Bix 7. The year 2022 marked the 48th running of the historic seven-mile race, geared to runners and walkers alike. The course, often attracting upwards of 12,000 participants, begins at the base of Brady Street Hill and is lined with live bands, cheering crowds, and often fun, costumed characters. Runners have included legends Bill Rodgers, Joan Benoit Samuelson, and Meb Keflezighi. Many winners have been from Kenya. Though the Bix 7 is named for the famous jazz cornetist and Davenport native Bix Beiderbecke, it has nothing to do with Bix and is separate from the Bix Beiderbecke Memorial Society and the Bix jazz fest held the following weekend.

Downtown Davenport, IA
bix7.com

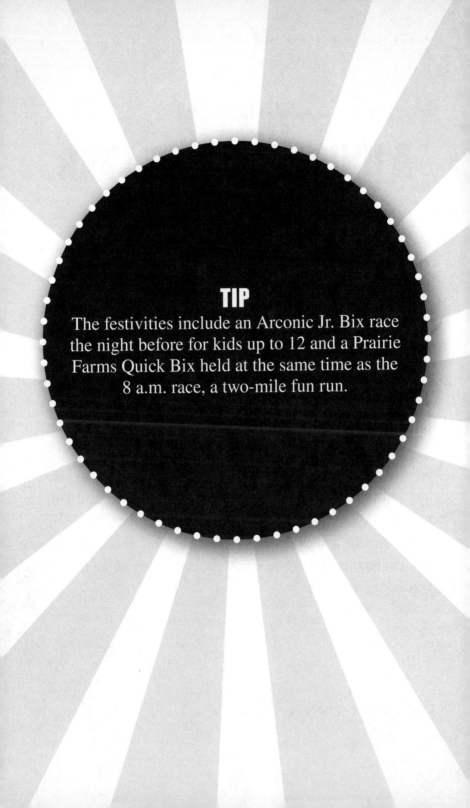

TIP

The festivities include an Arconic Jr. Bix race
the night before for kids up to 12 and a Prairie
Farms Quick Bix held at the same time as the
8 a.m. race, a two-mile fun run.

TAKE IN
A UNIQUE TUG-OF-WAR
AT TUG FEST

A uniquely QC event both binds and sets each side of the Mississippi against each other every August, with the big, rambunctious Tug Fest. As part of a three-day party in LeClaire, Iowa, and its cross-river neighbor, Port Byron, Illinois, ten 20-member teams pull a 2,700-foot and 680-pound rope spanning the Mississippi, competing for the traveling alabaster statue of a bald eagle. Since the event's founding in 1987 (through 2021), Port Byron has claimed the Tug Fest title 23 times. Over 35,000 people view this spectacular and only tug-of-war across the longest river in the nation. The feats of strength and endurance are complemented by parades, live music, food, carnival rides and games, one-mile and 5K fun runs, kids' games and kids' tug-of-war, a bags tournament, an arm-wrestling tournament, arts and crafts and other vendors, and huge fireworks. The pair of charming towns may be small, but everything about the Tug Fest is larger than life.

Downtown LeClaire, IA and Port Byron, IL
tugfest.com
tugfest.org

CLIMB TO A SPECTACULAR VIEW
AT SKYBRIDGE

If you want a brisk, easy workout, climb to the top of this eye-catching pedestrian bridge that spans River Drive in downtown Davenport. A local fitness club meets here Sundays at 9 a.m. Opened in 2005, the $7-million bridge spans from LeClaire Park to a courtyard and parking ramp on 2nd Street next to River Music Experience. The bridge is 50 feet tall and 575 feet long, with 99-foot-tall columns. Be sure to check it out at night, as the Skybridge contains 228 LED fixtures and 8,036 individual lights, displaying various patterns and colors through the year.

River Drive, near Main Street, Davenport, IA
neumannmonson.com/skybridge

Butterworth Center
Deere-Wiman House

CULTURE
AND HISTORY

STEP BACK IN TIME
AT THE BUTTERWORTH CENTER AND DEERE-WIMAN HOUSE

While John Deere is synonymous with Moline and the Quad Cities, his son Charles Deere was the driving force behind two of the most popular, impressive historic homes in the area. At the corner of Eleventh Avenue and Eighth Street in Moline are the gorgeous, stately Deere-Wiman House and Butterworth Center. Originally called Overlook for its hilltop location, the former was built by Charles in 1872 for his wife, Mary Little Dickinson Deere, and their daughters, serving as home for four generations of Deere descendants. First named Hillcrest, the latter was built in 1892 by Charles as a wedding gift for his youngest daughter, Katherine, and her husband, William Butterworth. Both homes have beautiful gardens.

The Butterworth Center
1105 8th St., Moline, IL, 309-743-2700

Deere-Wiman House
817 11th Ave., Moline, IL, 309-743-2718
butterworthcenter.com

TIP

At the Butterworth Center, be sure to see the library's 18th-century Italian ceiling painting, originally found in Venice and purchased by the Butterworths.

BE DAZZLED
AT THE PUTNAM MUSEUM
AND SCIENCE CENTER

Though the beloved Putnam was founded in 1867 as one of the first museums west of the Mississippi (in its present location since 1964), the sprawling facility has hardly been fixed in amber, but has been growing, changing, and progressing every year. The Putnam houses a mind-boggling 250,000 historical artifacts and specimens, a fraction of which are on display at any one time. Its Giant Screen Theater was added in 2002, and a Science Center created from existing space in 2014. An affiliate of the Smithsonian Institution, the museum has been home to blockbuster traveling exhibits devoted to the *Titanic* and *Princess Diana*, as well as invaluable homegrown displays, educating the public on the fascinating history and diversity of the area.

1717 W 12th St., Davenport, IA, 563-324-1933
putnam.org

TIP
Can't-miss permanent exhibits include a colorful World Culture Gallery, ancient Egyptian mummies, and a regional ecosystem gallery with an 850-gallon tank of Mississippi River fish.

FIND BLOOMS
AT THE QC BOTANICAL CENTER

The Botanical Center, which opened in 1998, is a phenomenal jewel inside and out, a premier destination for both children and adults, and a busy spot for club meetings and private events and receptions. The building's main attraction is a soaring Sun Garden, with a stunning 70-foot-tall skylight, 14-foot waterfall, stream, and fish pond that circulates water through the atrium, providing a home for popular Japanese Koi, and a wide range of plants. Outside, the grounds are meticulously maintained year-round, with a great variety of plants and flowers, and a whimsical children's garden that is an interpretation of the Mississippi River, including varied greenery, flowering perennials, and native prairie plants. There are interactive waterplay features as well.

2525 4th Ave., Rock Island, IL, 309-794-0991
qcgardens.com

TIP
An expansion of the children's garden including a replica of headwaters of the Mississippi opened in 2021.

FIND HOME IS WHERE ART IS
AT QUAD CITY ARTS

Like other arts organizations in the QC, Quad City Arts is more than a place; it's a force of nature. Serving a six-county area, the nonprofit has its headquarters in downtown Rock Island. This houses a chic gallery, store, and central office space. One of the best things the multi-faceted group does is present a vital, diverse Visiting Artist Series (for schools and community sites), including opportunities to meet some of the artists up close and personal in a Performing Arts Signature Series. In the 2021–22 school year alone, it had residencies and public performances from nine artists and ensembles, including a Syrian American funk/soul band, an Americana/classical string and vocal trio, a brass band, pianist, hip-hop/classical ballet troupe, and a Mexican folk/rock quintet. It also offers crucial grants to other artists and groups.

1715 2nd Ave., Rock Island, IL, 309-793-1213
quadcityarts.com

TIP
QC Arts leads a bountiful rotating public sculpture program and is beautifying further with many murals created by its Metro Arts program for local youth.

COMMUNE WITH NATURE AND HISTORY
AT BLACK HAWK STATE HISTORIC SITE

During COVID, a favorite family activity became walking the trails of the sprawling, beautiful Black Hawk State Historic Site in Rock Island. Overlooking the Rock River, the grounds include picnic areas and shelters with grills and fireplaces, an accessible lodge, museum, and paved trails, as well as 208 acres of public use areas, prairie, and a nature preserve with miles of marked hiking trails. The popular Watch Tower Lodge hosts weddings, receptions, business meetings, conferences, and dinners. It was designed by state architect Joseph Booton in 1932 and built entirely from local limestone and timber. Don't miss the John Hauberg Indian Museum at the west end of the lodge. It tells the story of the Sauk and Meskwaki people through interpretive maps, artifacts, and seasonal dioramas.

1510 46th Ave., Rock Island, IL, 309-788-0177
blackhawkpark.org

TIP
Take the free handheld audio tour and venture through an entire year with the last two Native American tribes who lived in the area.

SEE WHERE IT BEGAN
FOR ROCK ISLAND HAUBERGS

Without John Hauberg (1869-1955), there would be no Black Hawk State Park in Rock Island or the illuminating Native American museum on its grounds. Hauberg was a farm boy turned lawyer and one of the area's greatest philanthropists. The mansion he and his wife shared is a treasured estate that's open to the public.

In 1921, Hauberg persuaded the Illinois State legislature to purchase 200 acres of land that became Black Hawk State Historic Site, and in 1939 his collection of Indian artifacts made its debut in the museum that bears his name. The gorgeous Hauberg Estate was built in 1909-1911, for his wife, Susanne Denkmann, heiress of the Weyerhauser-Denkmann lumber fortune. Using Susanne's love of flowers as inspiration, architect Robert Spencer designed the Arts-and-Crafts place with tulips inside and out—in stained-glass windows, ceilings, tiles, and planters.

On the National Register of Historic Places, the elegant mansion (donated to the city in 1956 by the Hauberg children) consists of 20 rooms, six fireplaces, a carriage house stable, and garage. Volunteers have been tirelessly restoring the landscape and beautiful gardens, designed by noted architect Jens Jensen.

1300 24th St., Rock Island, IL, 309-373-5080
haubergestate.org

BE MERRY AND BRIGHT
AT THE KWIK STAR FESTIVAL OF TREES

The largest fundraiser for Quad City Arts, and a huge local attraction, the Kwik Star Festival of Trees takes over the Davenport RiverCenter for 11 days each year (the week before Thanksgiving, and the week of, but closed on the holiday). The seasonal explosion of color and light includes a CenterStage with talented local performers, Reindeer Games and Children's Activity Center, Festival Express, Gingerbread Village, art exhibits and galleries. There are also breathtaking designer displays of trees, wreaths, hearth and home, rooms, and holiday entries (all eligible for prizes), along with handcrafted ornaments, stockings, and trees featuring books and toys. The festival's Holiday Parade (on the first Saturday) is not only the largest helium balloon parade in the Midwest (with many inflated cartoon characters); it's also the only televised parade in the Quad-Cities.

136 E 3rd St., Davenport, IA, 309-793-1213
qcfestivaloftrees.com

TWO MORE BIG QUAD CITIES HOLIDAYS

St. Patrick's Grand Parade

For more than 35 years, each March the St. Patrick's Society of the Quad Cities has hosted the nation's only bi-state St. Patrick's Day parade. The day begins with a Mass in Rock Island, and the march starts downtown, traveling to the Talbot/Centennial Bridge, across the river to Davenport, and east through downtown Davenport, ending with a post-parade bash at the RiverCenter.
stpatsqc.com/grandparade.html

Red, White, and Boom!

Independence Day is annually celebrated with all-day, fun activities in Rock Island and Davenport on July 3. The fireworks which are in sync to music on 97X, are launched at 9:30 p.m. from two barges in the Mississippi River. Spectators can watch from viewing areas along the Davenport riverfront including LeClaire Park, Freight House Farmers Market parking lot, Quinlan Court and Bechtel Park, or Schwiebert Riverfront Park in downtown Rock Island.
redwhiteandboomqc.org

PAINT THE TOWN
WITH RIVERSSANCE
AND THE CHALK ART FEST

Quad City Arts also produces two outdoor art festivals. The first is Riverssance, known for its high-quality fine art, beautiful setting, and unique blend of entertainment, food, and wine. Located on a hill at Lindsay Park overlooking the Mississippi River in the historic Village of East Davenport, this two-day festival features over 70 artists, a children's art activity tent, wine tasting, food vendors, and live regional music. Awards are given to artists in various categories, and the prestigious Harley Award is given to an individual who's influenced the arts in the QC. The younger Chalk Art Fest is a two-day summer street event, where hundreds of artists transform blank cement pavement into incredible works of art. Visitors can watch, vote for their favorite, and do some chalk art of their own. Live music, a variety of food and drink vendors, and children's activities are all part of the festivities.

quadcityarts.com/riverssance-festival.html
quadcityarts.com/chalk-art-fest.html

CHECK OUT HISTORY
AT KARPELES MANUSCRIPT
LIBRARY MUSEUM

One of just 17 museums like it in the United States, the Karpeles in Rock Island is an imposing temple of learning in more ways than one. The massive building was formerly a Christian Science church, designed in the Palladian style and built between 1914 and 1915. Its exterior walls are of brick covered by Bedford limestone, with a front portico supported by six two-story columns with egg-and-dart capitals. Its dome actually consists of two domes: an outer dome and an inner dome separated by a space for lighting fixtures and maintenance. The inner dome consists of 8,000 colored fish-scale glass panes on a wooden support structure. The free museum has rotating exhibits from David and Marsha Karpeles, who own the largest private collection of historical documents in the world with over a million documents, plus books and drawings.

700 22nd St., Rock Island, IL, 309-788-0806
facebook.com/karpelesrockisland

CRUISE THROUGH HISTORY
ON THE *CHANNEL CAT*

Take a relaxing ride on the mighty Mississippi River and go back in time simultaneously with the *Channel Cat* water taxi and the new QC PastPort interactive service. The long established water taxi (typically running Memorial Day weekend through October) operates three open-air passenger ferryboats, with ports near Riverbend Commons by the Ben Butterworth Parkway, Moline; John Deere Commons behind the Radisson Hotel in Moline; The Isle Casino Hotel in Bettendorf; and Lindsay Park in the Village of East Davenport. Coming summer 2023 is a dock at the Bend in East Moline. Discover the cultural history of the QC with PastPort signs at each location, which feature instructions on how to join the digital tour on your smartphone through the Channel Cat App. All-day *Channel Cat* fares are $8 for adults and $4 for children 2–10.

metroqc.com/channelcat
qcpastport.com

MORE QUAD CITIES RIVER CRUISES

Celebration Belle
This is a beautiful 750-passenger, 4-deck riverboat, with two enclosed dining decks, two observation decks with outdoor seating, a gift shop, all meals freshly prepared on board, and entertainment.
2501 River Dr., Moline, IL, 800-297-0304
celebrationbelle.com

Riverboat *Twilight*
This replicated Victorian riverboat offers 90-minute cruises, as well as one-day and two-day river cruises. Meals are prepared on board in the lower galley, and a full bar and souvenir gift shop are available to enhance your experience.
197 N Front St., LeClaire, IA, 800-331-1467
riverboattwilight.com

American
This line serves the Upper Mississippi River with an 8-day, 7-night itinerary, including Davenport. It features a complimentary excursion shuttle at each stop.
800-460-4518
americancruiselines.com

Viking River Cruises
Viking began serving the Mississippi in 2022, with its first 386-guest custom vessel, offering sailings ranging from 8 to 15 days, including stops in Iowa in the QC, Burlington, and Dubuque.
855-338-4546
vikingcruises.com

CATCH A RISING COMIC
AT THE HISTORIC RENWICK MANSION

One of the most popular—and scenic—places to see stand-up comedy in the QC is the stunning Renwick Mansion. Launched in 2018, the Tomfoolery on Tremont series features comedians from New York to LA. The beautiful Davenport mansion was built in 1877 by William Renwick, who took over a lumber/sawmill business founded by his father, and is the city's finest example of Italian Revival Villa architecture. Sitting on four acres, the home features a large fourth-story tower that overlooks Davenport and the Mississippi River, wooden trim and twelve 14-foot doors, eight bedrooms available for rent, eight fireplaces, a three-story staircase, and a limestone exterior. Formerly part of a private school and later a nursing home, the Renwick has been extensively renovated, and since 2017 has served as a premier location for weddings, receptions, reunions, parties, and meetings. And many funny comics.

901 Tremont Ave., Davenport, IA, 563-484-0202
renwickmansion.net

DISCOVER QC SWEDISH HERITAGE
AT BISHOP HILL

Forty-one miles southeast of Moline, you can discover early QC history through the Bishop Hill Historic Site, celebrating the area's Swedish heritage. Bishop Hill—a hub for thousands of Swedish immigrants who eventually settled much of the Midwest—is much the same town you would have seen if you were in a horse and buggy 175 years ago: a fully functional, charming village. You can see the Bishop Hill Museum, Colony Church, Colony Hotel, and Village Park, open throughout the year and free for visitors. The museum and archives of the Bishop Hill Heritage Association are in the 1854 Steeple Building. Costumed interpreters are available to enhance your visit.

304 Bishop Hill St., Bishop Hill, IL, 309-927-3345
visitbishophill.com

TIP

At the nearby Bishop Hill Creative Commons, browse the art gallery which houses a wide array of fine art and traditional crafts made by local artists, attend a workshop, or check out a concert at the Commons. 309 N Bishop Hill Rd., Bishop Hill, IL, 309-927-3851, bishophillcommons.com

LEARN AN IMMIGRANT PAST
AT THE GERMAN AMERICAN HERITAGE CENTER

Davenport was once the most German city in Iowa, and you can find out why at the fascinating German American Heritage Center and Museum. A National Historic Site, the four-story brick building dates from the 1870s, when it was a hotel for thousands of German immigrants who flooded into the area. The museum (which opened in 2000) includes a large permanent exhibit and two rotating special exhibits. Within the permanent exhibit, there's an orientation theater, six education stations, and two restored hotel rooms. Using kiosks installed in 2021, interactively experience the immigrants' journeys by sea, train, and on foot to their final destination in Davenport. One highlight is where you can step onto the footprints of a child, female or male, and the program starts a corresponding character on a screen talking about his/her experience as an immigrant. The museum also provides workshops, educational programs, and classes.

712 W 2nd St., Davenport, IA, 563-322-8844
gahc.org

ADMIRE
THE EYE-CATCHING FIGGE ART MUSEUM

The Figge is as spectacularly impressive on the outside as the inside, and it is a treasured repository for art from around the world and for a voluminous amount of educational and public programming. Its stunning, sleek, glass building on the banks of the Mississippi, designed by British architect David Chipperfield, is home to a strong collection of American art, including 19th century and Midwest Regionalist works (like Iowa's Grant Wood) and presents first-class traveling exhibitions. The Figge studios, auditorium, and spacious lobby are alive with art classes, lectures, and special events that attract visitors of all ages. The $47-million building opened in 2005, and named in honor of a major gift from the V. O. and Elizabeth Kahl Figge Foundation. Its nearly 5,000 works of art include an extensive collection of Haitian, Colonial Mexican, and Midwestern art. In 1990, Grant Wood's estate, which included his personal effects and various works of art, became the property of the Figge.

225 W 2nd St., Davenport, IA, 563-326-7804
figgeartrmuseum.org

TIP
Be sure to also check out the Figge's wonderful café and elegant gift shop.

SALUTE AMERICAN VETERANS
ON HERO STREET

Hero Street in Silvis, Illinois, is a famous thoroughfare that honors veterans of World War II, Korea, and Vietnam. Just a block and a half long, Second Street in Silvis lost six young men in World War II and two in the Korean War, more than any other street in America. Hero Street has provided over 100 service members since Mexican American immigrants settled there in 1929. Admire the patriotic pride of the area at Hero Street Memorial Park and its impressive granite and bronze monument (dedicated in 2007) which stands over 17 feet tall, weighing 35 tons, honoring the eight Silvis heroes and all American veterans. Hero Street has been the subject of books and films, including a multi-part documentary series by Emmy-winning filmmakers Kelly and Tammy Rundle, that explore the compelling true story of Tony Pompa, Frank Sandoval, William Sandoval, Claro Solis, Peter Masias, Joseph Sandoval, Joseph Gomez, and John S. Muños.

145 2nd St., Silvis, IL
herostreetusa.org

GET A SENSE
OF THE SIZE AND SCOPE OF JOHN DEERE

Moline has been home to John Deere since 1847, and since 1997, the John Deere Pavilion downtown has been a hugely popular visitor attraction where they show off their tractors, sprayers, construction equipment, lawn tractors, and more. See new and vintage machines up close and explore interactive exhibits to discover how Deere's heritage and growth not only has developed the company, but has also impacted the world. Sit in the cab of some of John Deere's biggest machines, draw inspiration from stories of employees and customers, and learn from immersive exhibits with many touch-screen features. The 14,000-square-foot, glass-enclosed pavilion got an overhaul in 2021 and best of all, it's free!

1400 River Dr., Moline, IL
deere.com/en/connect-with-john-deere/visit-john-deere/pavilion

TIP
Also check out other must-see Deere properties in the area, including the renowned world headquarters, referred to as the "rusty palace," designed by Eero Saarinen, and the John Deere Historic Site in Grand Detour, Illinois, 72 miles northeast of Moline.

HANG OUT WITH THE ANIMALS
AT NIABI ZOO

Family fun is guaranteed at Niabi Zoo, operated by the Rock Island County Forest Preserve District. On over 40 acres, the zoo cares for more than 800 animals representing 200 species from around the world. With its education programs and unique guest experiences, Niabi also provides superb animal care for 26 species that are endangered. Niabi is at the forefront of conservation of species and habitats through local efforts as well as partners around the world. Take in a train, a carousel, and giraffe feedings twice a day (Passport to Africa includes a male giraffe and a female that guests may feed under staff supervision). Inside the giraffe house is a mixed primate exhibit, featuring Azul, a Wolf's Guenon, and Azizi, an Allen's Swamp Monkey. Nearby are zebras, ostriches, aldabra tortoises Charlotte and Wilbur, and Gabe the Dromedary. Niabi is open from April through October, and you can take a virtual tour anytime online.

13010 Niabi Zoo Rd., Coal Valley, IL, 309-799-3482
niabizoo.com

TAKE IN THE OPULENCE
OF THE PALMER MANSION

B.J. Palmer's home in Davenport is as colorful and eccentric as he was. The second head of Palmer College of Chiropractic, founded by his father, D.D., B.J. Palmer (1882–1961) was an Odd Fellow and a Mason—both fraternal charitable organizations. The Palmer Mansion was built in 1874 and is a staggering cross between Graceland and the House on the Rock. Palmer loved cigars, music, the circus, the Civil War era, dressing to the nines, books, traveling, swords, and radio, and the house reflects all these interests. Among its many fascinating pieces are Asian artwork, an Oriental solarium, chess sets with detailed carved ivory pieces, and a 1922 pipe organ with over 1,000 pipes.

808 Brady St., Davenport, IA, 563-884-5714
palmer.edu

TIP

Chiropractic care was invented in Davenport in 1895, and the Palmer Foundation for Chiropractic History has historical displays located throughout the three Palmer campuses, including Florida and California.

PAY TRIBUTE
TO THE ARMED FORCES
AT THE ROCK ISLAND ARSENAL

It's hard to overstate the importance of the Rock Island Arsenal to the Quad Cities area. An active US Army facility, headquarters of the First Army, it's on a 946-acre island on the Mississippi River, and houses the largest government-owned manufacturing facility in the US. Its many historical attractions include the Rock Island Arsenal Museum, Colonel Davenport House, Memorial Park, Mississippi River Visitors Center, Rock Island National Cemetery, a Confederate Cemetery, and Quarters One (formerly the second-largest residence in the federal government, next only to the White House).

Rock Island Arsenal, IL
Enter from Moline Gate off River Dr.
home.army.mil/ria/index.php

TIP
The fascinating Colonel Davenport House (on the northern edge of the island) dates from 1833 and has been renovated over the years. It was the home of George Davenport, one of the main settlers of the area, who was murdered in the home in 1845.

ATTRACTIONS NEAR THE ARSENAL

Government Bridge
The 1896 Government Bridge (connecting Arsenal Island
to Davenport) is a double-decker bridge with sets of
railroad tracks above and a roadway below, and it has a
swing span that can rotate 360 degrees in either direction,
allowing river traffic to pass through. This combination
makes the bridge the only one of its kind in the US.
iowadot.gov/autotrails/government-bridge

Bechtel Park
On the Davenport side of the bridge, visit Bechtel Park
and its impressive, imposing bronze sculpture of Abraham
Lincoln. The Bechtel Trusts commissioned Illinois artist
Jeff Adams to honor Lincoln's involvement in the famous
lawsuit filed by owners of the *Effie Afton* steamboat, which
struck the original railroad bridge nearby in 1856, the first
span to cross the 2,230-mile-long Mississippi. Lincoln was
part of the Chicago legal team that defended the bridge
owners. The 15-foot-high, 3,100-pound sculpture depicts
the future president and the son of the lead bridge engineer.
2nd St., west of Iowa St., Davenport, IA

HAVE A
WILD TIME LEARNING
AT THE BUFFALO BILL MUSEUM

One of the QC's most famous natives was William "Buffalo Bill" Cody (1846–1917), born in LeClaire. He was a frontiersman, US Army Scout, and later a showman touring throughout the United States and Europe with his Wild West Congress show. The Buffalo Bill Museum on the LeClaire riverfront showcases his life, early history, documents, and relics pertaining to the Mississippi River, Native Americans, early American life and settlers, and the connection with LeClaire and Scott County. Built in 1868, the *Lone Star* stern-wheeler is the only surviving example in the nation of a wooden-hulled boat built in the Western Rivers fashion. The museum also focuses on artifacts and records of LeClaire families such as household items, clothing, and personal effects. It also has a re-creation of a one-room schoolhouse accompanied by records from the school, manufacturing exhibits, and Indian and prehistoric artifacts.

199 N Front St., LeClaire, IA, 563-289-5580
buffalobillmuseumleclaire.com

JOIN IN THE FUN
AT THE COLORFUL FAMILY MUSEUM

The two-story-high ceiling across the lobby of the Family Museum in Bettendorf is a gorgeous explosion of color, and that same energy and rainbow of experiences pulses through the city-owned center (part of the Learning Campus, next to the public library). Not only home to a variety of classes, camps, an Imagination Studio, and outdoor play area, this innovative museum has permanent hands-on exhibits including the town of Fox Hollow, George's Farm, a river valley where you can explore the mighty Mississippi on a small scale (with waterplay and bridges), and a playhouse and virtual pond for kids four and under.

2900 Learning Campus Dr., Bettendorf, IA, 563-344-4106
familymuseum.org

TIP
See the two-story climber in the Great Hall made of large platforms surrounded by a secure vinyl-coated cable netting. This artistically stunning structure allows guests to climb from the first floor to the second while observing photos of clouds. You can scale many heights (physically and mentally) in this museum.

ADMIRE UNIQUE, BEAUTIFUL CEMETERIES
AT CHIPPIANNOCK AND RIVERSIDE

Cemeteries usually aren't visitor destinations beyond family and friends of those resting there, but two in the Illinois QC are well worth seeing. The sprawling, hilly Chippiannock in Rock Island is the final resting place of many interesting, influential people from all walks of life—everyone from QC settler George Davenport to local musician Ellis Kell. The monuments, grave markers, and mausolea that serve as focal points for panoramic vistas in the landmark's grounds are fascinating. Life-size stone statues and ship's anchors join six-ton granite balls and babies' cradles among more memorable markers. Located at Riverside in Moline on a high hill overlooking the river, with unique terracing, this cemetery houses the remains of 28,000 people, including legendary drummer Louie Bellson; inventor, industrialist, and one-time Moline Mayor John Deere; other members of the Deere family; and even Charles Dickens's son, Francis.

Chippiannock Cemetery
2901 12th St., Rock Island, IL
chippiannock.com

Riverside Cemetery
3400 5th Ave., Moline IL
moline.il.us/263/riverside-cemetery

TAKE A "BRAKE"
AT THE WORLD'S LARGEST TRUCKSTOP

The QC is the only place I-80 meets the Mississippi River, and it's fitting you can take a "brake" at the World's Largest Truckstop and Iowa 80 Trucking Museum. The museum collection was started by Truckstop founder Bill Moon, who clearly had a passion for trucks. The museum—which tracks the evolution of the industry—has over 100 antique trucks on display, as well as 304 original petroliana signs and 24 vintage gas pumps. Many rare and one-of-a-kind trucks are there, and you can see short films about trucking history in the REO theater. The Iowa 80 Truckstop itself is a small city (founded in 1964), open 24/7, featuring eight restaurants, a convenience store, gift store, Super Truck Showroom, barber shop, chiropractor, dentist, movie theater, workout room, laundry facilities, gas islands, diesel fuel center, truck service center, truck wash, pet wash, and 24 private showers.

I-80 Exit 284, Walcott, IA
iowa80truckstop.com
iowa80truckingmuseum.com

SEE A SIMPLER TIME
AT THE PIONEER VILLAGE

Go back in time at Scott Country Park in Dan Nagle Walnut Grove Pioneer Village, once a county cross-roads settlement and stagecoach stop of the 1860s. The Village includes 22 historic buildings, some relocated. Olde St. Ann's Church is a restored 1870s church available for weddings. Main Street has a little bit of everything. Like all small-town general stores, Keppy & Nagle was the gathering place for everyone. The boardwalk takes visitors to the doctor's office, fire station, barber shop, and even jail. Step into the soda fountain on summer weekends to have a taste of the past. There are events with period demonstrators, summer day camp, self-guided tours, and picnicking.

18817 290th St., Long Grove, IA, 563-328-3283
scottcountyiowa.gov/conservation/pioneer-village

TIP

The 1,280-acre Scott County Park has 14 picnic areas and shelters with tables, grills and/or fireplaces, as well as a baseball field, playground equipment, nature trails, an equestrian area, and five unique camping areas.

Photo courtesy of Argrow's House of Healing and Hope

SHOPPING
AND FASHION

TRY ON VINTAGE CLOTHES AND JEWELRY
AT ABERNATHY'S

There are few stores in the Quad Cities that are as quirky, weird, and downright delightful as Abernathy's in downtown Davenport. They specialize in true vintage clothing for men and women from the 1930s to the mid-'60s, modern vintage reproduction clothing in all sizes, alternative and gothic styles, handmade jewelry and art, antiques, oddities, and home décor. Abernathy's was started in 2013 by Becca Nicke and Red Perez, who previously worked managing a vintage and handmade boutique in LeClaire. They opened their first location on East 2nd Street in downtown Davenport but were flooded in spring 2019. The new store re-opened in August 2019 in a beautiful historic building, allowing them to feature more new products than ever and expanding their reach in the QC and worldwide.

432 W 3rd St., Davenport, IA, 563-650-9463
shopabernathys.com

TIP

Be sure to check out the similarly funky Doodads next door, with delightfully different, affordable antiques, furniture, jewelry, retro relics, and gifts.

LINGER IN THE '50S
AT FRED & ETHEL'S

If you love the 1950s, then you must check out Fred & Ethel's '50s Retro Antiques store. Owner Jennifer Horvath has vintage merchandise in her blood. She was inspired to open in 2000, after growing up with her mother's antique store and her grandparents' 1950s-style ranch house. She loves kitsch, bright, cheery fun stuff, specializing in all those mid-century items that you love: retro clothing and jewelry, kitchen items, housewares, cocktail and barware, vintage Christmas, and lots more. The store is lovingly named for Fred and Ethel Mertz (the neighbors in the '50s classic TV show *I Love Lucy*), and Horvath also stocks items from the '60s and '70s. Babaloo!

1326 30th St., Rock Island, IL, 309-786-3511
facebook.com/fredandethelsretro

PERUSE VINTAGE
AT RAGGED RECORDS
AND TRASH CAN ANNIE'S

Bob Herington and Laura Heath share an "old-soul" vibe. They are expert curators of America's past—in music and fashion, with Herington's Ragged Records and Heath's Trash Can Annie's sharing a downtown Davenport space since summer 2021. Until that time, each had run his/her own store nearby, both of which were ruined by the 2019 flood. Ragged (which opened a Rock Island location in 2018) features 30,000 new and used vinyl records, as well as thousands of CDs. Heath's impeccable fashion taste—highlighted by clothes, accessories, and other items mainly from 1870-1970—has brought her jobs costuming for TV, film, and Broadway, including the Netflix series *Hollywood* and the 1997 blockbuster *Titanic*. She offers styling and photography, and Herington also sells audio equipment, including turntables, speakers, and accessories like guitar strings, audio cords, and batteries. It's all music to shoppers' and environmentalists' ears—recycling, reusing, and repurposing beauty.

311 E 2nd St., Davenport, IA
Ragged: 563-324-3579
raggedrecords.com

Trash Can Annie: 563-322-5893
trashcanannie.com

SHOP
AMERICAN PICKERS
AT ANTIQUE ARCHAEOLOGY

In 1987, little LeClaire was put on the national map with the launch of the summertime Tug Fest, the only tug-of-war across the Mississippi River. In 2010, the town got greater attention with the launch of the History cable series *American Pickers*, started by pals Mike Wolfe and Frank Fritz (Bettendorf natives), and you can pick your own unique items at their Antique Archaeology business. This former fabrication shop is home to *American Pickers* and houses some of their best picks as well as a new merchandise store. The diverse products include antiques, Two Lanes and Antique Archaeology gear (like shirts and caps), signs, magnets, koozies, license plates, keychains, pins, drinkware, and home goods. Wolfe also runs a similar store in Nashville, Tennessee, with vintage items, collectibles, and unique home décor.

115½ Davenport St., LeClaire, IA, 563-265-3939
antiquearchaeology.com

TAKE BEAUTIFUL POTTERY FOR A SPIN
AT DOT'S POTS

Dot's Pots in Moline is a beloved store featuring functional, fun, and whimsical pottery created by Dorothy "Dot" Beach-Lawrence and her husband, Dan Lawrence. The couple has been making functional, beautiful, and quirky clay products for more than 30 years. They include items like pitchers, dinnerware, and flower pots, and are microwave-safe. Dot also creates wonderful Raku pottery. Dot's Pots was the only QC business to be chosen in 2021 among 28 small companies across Illinois in the Illinois Made program by the state's Office of Tourism. The program recognizes each business as a "hidden gem for locals and visitors to discover, offering unique products and experiences." Dot's store features mugs, plates, trays, vases, miniatures, ornaments, and very cute earrings.

2822 16th St., Moline, IL, 309-736-7247
facebook.com/molinepotters

GET SOME GREEN
AT THE JOHN DEERE STORE

Contrary to what Kermit the Frog sang, it IS easy being green at the John Deere Store, right across from the phenomenal John Deere Pavilion in Deere's hometown of Moline. The agricultural, construction, lawn, and turf equipment giant not only has plants around the world but fans everywhere who love the brand and the leaping-deer logo. That iconic look is spread everywhere in the store—the possibilities appear limitless, in merchandise for men, women, and kids. Of course, there are Deere hats and T-shirts, but also polo shirts, button-downs, sweatshirts, hoodies, jackets, sweaters and outerwear, belts and buckles, wallets, handbags, accessories, toys, collectibles, mugs, glassware, prints, books, games, puzzles, and other items for children ages infant through teens.

1300 River Dr., Moline, IL, 309-765-1007
johndeerestore.com

HOP ON OVER TO CHARM
AT GRASSHOPPERS

You could spend a day absorbing all the charm and sophistication in downtown LeClaire, and a good part of that is due to Grasshoppers Gift Shop and Guest Houses. Monica Schons, owner of the gift-shop side of the business, has her own flair and personality. In addition to LeClaire's beautiful view of the Mississippi River, the shop offers wonderful gifts, interesting antiques, and painted furniture. You'll find goodies like home décor, wines and spirits, stylish women's clothing, and lots of unique jewelry (many of the pieces made by Monica herself). The basement of the gift shop features the Captain's Spirit Cellar, with its variety of great wines and fun labels, along with wine accessories. Be sure to check out the nearby guest houses, available for lodging.

208 N Cody Rd., LeClaire, IA, 563-289-4652
shopthehop.com
visitleclaire.com

TIP
There are 60 buildings that comprise the Cody Road District in LeClaire, including incredible restaurants, amazing events, and unique boutique shopping.

ADMIRE SHOPPING VARIETY
AT WATERMARK CORNERS

WaterMark Corners is one of the most distinctive gift shops in the area, a longtime gift and stationery store in a beautiful historic building in downtown Moline, owned by a dynamic mother-daughter duo, Barbara and Amy Trimble. They travel all over to find new items that are innovative, intriguing, and inspiring, and their unique, varied, and constantly updated merchandise reflects their passion. The inviting store includes QC-themed gifts, pet gifts, loungewear, drinkware, gourmet kitchen items, jewelry, greeting cards, bath and body items, apparel, games, puzzles, and tech accessories. In 2017, *Forbes* named them among the top Main Street businesses in the country for their innovative approach to using Facebook for marketing.

1500 River Dr., Moline, 309-764-0055
watermarkcorners.com

TIP

In late 2021, the Trimbles opened the
Corner Bar in the store, not only with shelves
full of wine and related items, but a bar menu
with wines, beers, sodas, cider, cocktails,
and frozen cocktail slushies by the glass,
as well as to-go mixes.

SNAG A CONCRETE CREATION
AT ISABEL BLOOM

The name Isabel Bloom is one of the best-known in the QC, as both the beloved artist (1908–2001) and the longtime business that bears her name. She studied at Iowa's Stone City Art Colony under American master Grant Wood in the '30s, and her concrete sculptures evoked simple shapes and rounded features, often depicting children, animals, and mother/child motifs. Her processes of wet cement casting, finishing, and coating remain virtually the same in the company's Davenport production studio. You can take free tours and see the detailed, painstaking process that goes into every sculpture. There are exclusive tour pieces and some more popular designs, available for purchase at the conclusion of the tour.

736 Federal St., Davenport, IA, 563-336-3766
ibloom.com

TIP

The annual Village in Bloom arts festival, honoring Isabel and her husband John Bloom, is free and held in the Village of East Davenport typically in May.

FIND CLOTHES THAT MAKE THE MAN (AND WOMAN)
AT THE GENTRY SHOP

A plush home of class and sophistication, The Gentry Shop has offered the highest quality clothing in the Quad Cities since 1948. It boasts the most extensive collection of the finest clothes, with expert tailoring and unmatched personalized service. Menswear includes custom-tailored and made-to-measure suits, sport coats, slacks, shirts, shorts, sportswear, and formal wear. Their full lines of women's clothes includes dresses, blouses, skirts, slacks, sportswear, accessories, and footwear. The Gentry Shop prides itself on wardrobe consultation and on-site master tailoring.

5515 Utica Ridge Rd., Davenport, IA, 563-324-6689
thegentryshop.com

JOIN THE COLORFUL DIVERSITY
OF MERCADO ON FIFTH

The lively, irresistible Mercado on Fifth hosts vibrant outdoor markets every Friday during the summer on Fifth Avenue in Moline. The family-friendly events feature a wide variety of food trucks, mobile boutiques and retail vendors, children's activities, and live music and entertainment. The nonprofit works with both English and Spanish-speaking entrepreneurs to help start and grow their businesses. Starting in 2022, a new indoor community space with 6,300 square feet indoors and 5,000 square feet of patio space opens for year-round programming and events. Mercado on Fifth draws a diverse crowd, defines a sense of community and cultural pride, and creates a connection between the Hispanic Floreciente neighborhood and Moline's downtown.

5th Avenue between 12th and 11th streets, Moline, IL, 305-934-5297
mercadoonfifth.org

INDULGE IN WINE AND MUSIC
AT THE GRAPE LIFE

There's nowhere in the QC like the relaxing, rejuvenating sanctuary that is the Grape Life Wine Store & Lounge. Run by the passionate couple Diane and Kevin Koster, they offer a staggering variety of wonderful wines from all over the world, plus wine by the glass or taste flight, and some nice appetizers. The Grape Life carries great wine gift items and gift cards, and offers a wide range of amazing local musicians performing on most Friday and Saturday nights. You can join them for the popular "Wine Down" every Wednesday from 5 p.m.-8 p.m., where you can get a $6 glass of wine and a free chair massage from a massage therapist.

3402 Elmore Ave., Davenport, IA, 563-355-7070
thegrapelife.com

TIP

Be sure to check out the very cool counter at the bar, where there are dozens of corks on display under the glass.

FIND IT ALL
AT FREIGHT HOUSE FARMERS MARKET

One of the places to be on summer weekends is the great Freight House Farmers Market on the lovely Mississippi riverfront in downtown Davenport. The wide variety represents friendly regional producers from many counties across Iowa and Illinois, offering locally produced fresh fruit and vegetables, eggs, meat, cheese, herbs, flowers and plants, honey, wine, hand-crafted items, a variety of ready-to-eat foods, and more. The Freight House Farmers Market supports nearly 200 farmers, crafters, and artisan food entrepreneurs. In addition to shopping for fresh produce and more, visitors can take in live entertainment and enjoy the atmosphere. The indoor market operates year-round on Saturdays 8 a.m.-2 p.m. and Sundays 10 a.m.-2 p.m., and the outdoor market is a rain-or-shine event that runs from early May through the last weekend in October (Wednesdays 4 p.m.-8 p.m., Saturdays 8 a.m.-2 p.m. and Sundays 10 a.m.-2 p.m.).

421 W River Dr., Davenport, IA, 563-770-FHFM
freighthousefarmersmarket.com

WHILE YOU'RE AT THE FREIGHT HOUSE, CHECK OUT THESE EATERIES

Front Street Brewery & Taproom
Since 2012, the main brewing operations of Front Street Brew Pub (the oldest brew pub in Iowa, opening in 1992) have been here.
421 W River Dr., Davenport, IA, 563-324-4014
frontstreetbrew.com/taproom

Antonella's
A longtime Davenport favorite, here you can get authentic Sicilian cuisine and an unbeatable river view.
421 W River Dr., Davenport, IA, 563-324-9512
antonellas2.com

The Diner
On the second floor of the 1917 Freight House, the Diner is a favorite breakfast and lunch spot, with no bad selection on the extensive, comfort-food laden menu.
421 W River Dr., Davenport, IA, 563-323-0895
thedinerqc.com

Chill Ice Cream & Eats
In addition to premium ice cream, you can chill here with tasty burgers, loaded fries, Iowa cheese curds, handmade pretzels, and more from locally sourced ingredients.
421 W River Dr., Davenport, IA, 563-271-4960
chillicecreamandeats.com

Taste of Ethiopia
This wonderful restaurant grew out of the Farmers Market and opened in 2019. The only Ethiopian eatery in the area, its authentic dishes are prepared with care and spice.
102 S Harrison St., Davenport, IA, 563-424-1848
tasteofethiopiaqc.com

REVEL IN
GREAT REGIONAL ART
AT QUAD CITY ARTS GALLERY

The Quad City Arts Gallery in downtown Rock Island is home to rotating exhibits of talented local and regional artists. The gallery space, once a turn-of-the-century department store, features hardwood floors and a 14-foot-high ceiling. The exhibition space is more than 1,500 square feet, a perfect place to showcase large paintings and sculptures and enjoy an occasional performance. A highlight for each exhibit is a lively opening reception, with complimentary wine and cheese.

1715 2nd Ave., Rock Island, IL, 309-793-1213
quadcityarts.com

TIP

Be sure to check out the gallery store for one-of-a-kind, priceless gifts, crafted with care by 75 local and regional artists working in just about any medium.

MORE OUTSTANDING QUAD CITIES ART GALLERIES

Augustana Teaching Museum of Art
639 38th St., Rock Island, IL
augustana.edu/locations/augustana-teaching-museum-art

Catich and Morrissey Galleries
518 W Locust St., Davenport, IA, 563-333-6444
(at St. Ambrose University) IA
sau.edu/catich

Hot Glass
104 Western Ave., Davenport, IA, 309-236-9223
hotglassart.org

Quad City Arts Art @ the Airport
Quad City Arts' gallery at QC International Airport is
across from the gift shop and restaurant and right before
the security checkpoint. The gallery never closes, and you
will pay just a dollar for parking.
2200 69th Ave., Moline, IL, 309-757-1768
qcairport.com/airport-guide/art-gallery

Smith Studio and Gallery
124 S State St., Geneseo, IL, 309-945-5428
smithstudiogeneseo.com

RutabagA
108 N State St., Geneseo, IL, 309-944-4994
rutabagaart.com

BROWSE
BIG-CITY TRENDS
AT URBAN FARMHOUSE

Urban Farmhouse began as a tiny shop with a big heart. The friendly folks at UF pride themselves on offering "everything you need for yourself or for a gift," including fragrances, home décor, bath/body products, drinkware, kitchen and entertaining goods, books/journals, jewelry, stationery, cards, and much more. They say shopping at UF isn't about the merchandise, it's about the feeling. They encompass five store locations (including Black Sheep Clothier and The Ugly Duckling) under the homespun UF brand, and if you can't find something unique and special at any of them, you're really not trying very hard.

208 S State St., Geneseo, IL, 309-714-5301
1209 4th Ave., Suite 1, Moline, IL, 309-524-3069
216 Sycamore St., Muscatine, IA, 563-316-0139
theufbrand.com

FIND SOMETHING THAT SUITS YOUR STYLE
AT THEO & CO.

Where can you find an upscale men's clothing store and a meticulous barber in one place? You can at Theo & Co., where QC native Annie Stopulos created a shopping experience unlike anything else in the area. She wanted guys to be able to come in, grab a drink, relax, and shop in a laid back, rustic-industrial vibe with soft music and sports on TV in the custom lounge. The store sells a thoughtfully curated collection of ready-to-wear clothing, leather goods, shoes, gifts, and accessories. Cool products include QC-branded hats and T-shirts and an 11-ounce glass etched with the streets and neighborhoods of Davenport. In 2020, Jeff Hankins, owner of the Gentlemen's Barber Shop and Shave Parlor, opened up inside Theo & Co.

219 E 2nd St., Davenport, IA, 563-232-6164
theoandcoshop.com

SUPPORT WOMEN WITH BEAUTY
AT ARGROW'S HOUSE

A profoundly special store in the QC is Argrow's House of Healing and Hope. Founder Dr. Kit Evans-Ford named the store after her grandmother, Rev. Argrow Margaret Warren, who lived through a violent marriage but embodied compassion and courage. There are free services offered daily at Argrow's House for women in the area recovering from violence and abuse. To help empower women in mind, body, and spirit as well as financially, Evans-Ford launched a business making bath and body products, where her clients create beautiful, all-natural soaps, shampoos, lotions, body washes, and more, providing a living wage for themselves in a safe space that celebrates who they are.

2313 44th St., Moline, IL, 563-528-0892
argrowshouse.org

TIP
If you can't luxuriate in the intoxicating scents of the store in person (its limited hours are Wednesday and Saturday 10 a.m.-2 p.m.), check out their website 24 hours a day.

CAPTURE CHARM
AT PLAID RABBIT
AND MEZZANINE BOUTIQUE

In the charming, easily walkable Village of East Davenport, two of the many fun destinations share an address—the quirky Plaid Rabbit and stylish Mezzanine Boutique. The former carries a wide assortment of gifts to celebrate life events like weddings, graduations, and births. They also have beautiful items to give as host/hostess gifts and for bridal showers and other types of entertaining, as well as classy, high-quality stationery, announcements, and invitations. The Mezzanine (a women's clothing boutique) carries a lovely assortment of blouses, dresses, skirts, denim, jewelry, accessories, shoes, and home gifts such as candles, drinkware, bath products, and more.

1026 Mound St., Davenport, IA
Plaid Rabbit: 563-324-9224
villageplaidrabbit.com
Mezzanine: 563-349-7231
mezzanineboutique.com

TIP

While you're in the Village, check out the variety of restaurants and unique stores, as well as a few of my favorite hangouts—Camp McClellan Cellars, Village Theatre, and Lindsay Park, one of the prettiest in the area, with a gorgeous view of the Mississippi.

MAKE NO BONES
ABOUT SKELETON KEY
ART AND ANTIQUES

Skeleton Key Art and Antiques is a unique store in a very different venue. The historic building was formerly a residence and funeral home, but for several years has been a homey, bountifully varied shopping destination. Over 100 vendors sell a stunning collection of art, antiques, crafts, gift ideas, and more. With jewelry, candles, fine antiques, furniture, and original art filling 6,000 square feet of retail space, Skeleton Key Art and Antiques aims to offer something for everyone. And you will likely find it.

520 18th St., Rock Island, IL, 309-314-1567
skeletonkeyqc.com

TIP

The local mall typically hosts an outdoor Artists' Market on selected Sundays in summer months. You can buy art directly from the artist who created it, learn about their process, and mix and mingle with neighbors and fellow art lovers.

ACTIVITIES
BY SEASON

FALL

Cross Four Cities and Two States in Quad Cities Marathon, 61

See a Simpler Time at the Pioneer Village, 106

Commune with Nature and History at Black Hawk State Historic Site, 84

Paint the Town with Riverssance and the Chalk Art Fest, 88

Admire a Unique Park at Sylvan Island, 72

WINTER

Be Merry and Bright at the Kwik Star Festival of Trees, 86

Slide into Family Fun at Snowstar, 66

Be Dazzled at the Putnam Museum and Science Center, 81

Thrill to Hockey with the Quad City Storm, 68

SPRING

Find Blooms at the QC Botanical Center, 82

Hear the Bats Crack at Modern Woodmen Park, 70

Look for Indoor Spikes with the QC Steamwheelers, 69

Hang Out with the Animals at Niabi Zoo, 98

SUMMER

• •

SUGGESTED
ITINERARIES

EXERCISE GOOD JUDGEMENT OUTDOORS

GET IN TUNE WITH MUSIC HOT SPOTS

TRACK DOWN ENTERTAINING THEATERS

• •

MAKE HISTORY AT THESE FAMOUS SITES

OH SAY, CAN YOU SEE THESE GREAT VIEWS?

BE A GOOD SPORT WITH THESE FUN AND GAMES

• •

INDEX

• •

• •

• •